BROADCAST JOURNALISM
Basic Principles

BROADCAST JOURNALISM

Basic Principles

S.C. BHATT

Published by Ashok Gosain and Ashish Gosain for
HAR-ANAND PUBLICATIONS PVT LTD
E-49/3, Okhla Industrial Area, Phase-II, New Delhi-110020
Tel.: 41603490
E-mail: info@haranandbooks.com/haranand@rediffmail.com
Shop online at: www.haranandbooks.com

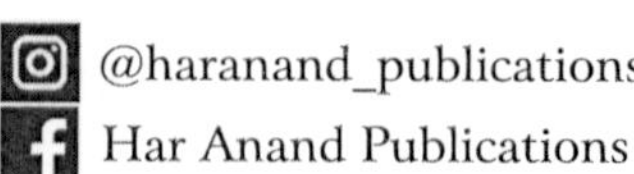

Reprint, 2025

PREFACE

The electronic media have become a part of our life and their role is increasing in importance day by day. The field of broadcast journalism is expanding likewise. In India and other countries, in South Asia and in South - East Asia the media are occupying a significant position. This is bound to become more important and relevant in the years to come.

More and more young men and women are aspiring to make a career in broadcast journalism. The number of those seeking admission to schools of journalism and institutions of mass communication is rising. Facilities, specially in terms of the quality of education imparted, are, however, not keeping pace with this growing interest.

Communication education, more than any other discipline of learning, needs to be based on sufficiently high level of work experience. It would not be an exaggeration to say that only those individuals who have gone through the mill and acquired experience and insight into the media and some mastery over the skills of communication can pass on their experience to the young aspirants. Ability to communicate the experience can be a useful tool. But a teacher who relies mainly on books would lack depth and be unsure of what he is teaching.

The situation is further complicated by the fact that often books addressed to the students in developed countries are relied on by such teachers. Admittedly, there has been a dearth of good books on journalism, particularly broadcast journalism, written with the Indian and other Asian students in view.

Years ago, as a member of the founding faculty of the Indian Institute of Mass Communication (IIMC), Delhi, I had developed a series of lessons on broadcast journalism for several batches of trainees of the Central Information Service, now known as Indian Information Service. Many of these trainees are now occupying top or middle level echelons in the electronic media. Exigencies of work in the service, to which I also belonged, took me back to active work which only helped me to enrich my experience of the media. But the IIMC kept beckoning me and I deem it my good fortune that I returned to (occasional) teaching as I was invited to lecture to broadcast journalism classes.

The book thus represents not only the essence of a lifetime of experience in broadcast media but also years of imparting that experience to young people.

The work is offered to all aspirants to a career in broadcast journalism, students of the various schools of journalism as well as to the practitioners in the media. The latter will find in the book useful tips to help them better their skills and understand the rationale of their work, the rules and guidelines.

Since news writing for the broadcast media is essentially an exercise in good writing, the print media journalists may also benefit by a study of this book. For the general reader interested in the intricacies of broadcast journalism and the problem of media credibility it may not be unrewarding to go through the book.

Teaching, I discovered long ago, means considerable learning. Many of the ideas propounded in this book were formulated in the course of teaching at the IIMC. My thanks are thus due to a number of batches of trainees whom I was privileged to teach. I must also acknowledge the material received from Bibekanand Ray, Additional Director General, News Services Division of All India Radio, a friend and a former student. I thank him and AIR for allowing me to use some of their bulletins in this book.

S.C. BHATT

CONTENTS

LIST OF ABBREVIATIONS

AFP	:	Agence France Press
AIDS	:	Acquired Immuno Deficiency Syndrome
AIR	:	All India Radio
ANC	:	African National Congress
AP	:	Associated Press
BBC	:	British Broadcasting Corporation
BJP	:	Bhartiya Janata Party
CBI	:	Central Bureau of Investigation
CCPA	:	Cabinet Committee for Political Affairs
CO	:	Crowd out
CPI (M)	:	Communist Party of India (Marxist)
CWC	:	Congress Working Committee
GNR	:	General News Room
GOC	:	General Overseas Service
JD	:	Janata Dal
JP	:	Janata Party
JPC	:	Joint Parliamentary Committee
NEHU	:	North Eastern Hill University
PDIC	:	Public Demands Implementation Convention
PMO	:	Prime Minister's Office
PTC	:	Part Time Correspondents
PTI	:	Press Trust of India
RSS	:	Rashtriya Swayam Sevak Sangh
SAARC	:	South Asian Association of Regional Co-operation
UN	:	United Nations
UNI	:	United News of India
UP	:	Uttar Pradesh
US	:	United States

Chapter I

THE NATURE OF NEWS

The hunger for knowing the latest relevant information is insatiable. It is expressed in the very words of greetings we use, in our different languages, when we meet friends "What News? "What's New?" "Anything fresh and new'!" are some of these forms in which people greet one another and which convey a desire to know the latest.

Often the substance may be missing and only the form may remain but the underlying truth—the urge to know the latest—cannot be denied.

What response do we expect to get when we ask a friend, a busybody in the office or a knowall: "What is the news''? Our expectation generally is that person would tell us something new and also something *interesting*. What we already know is not *news* to us. So also what an audience of the radio or TV or a newspaper reader already knows is not news to it.

The information has got to be interesting too. Certain things like a national crisis or a development of nationwide significance is of interest to a wide body of listeners and viewers. Other events may have limited significance. The prices of potatoes rising or falling cannot by itself become news. But a sudden spurt in prices may exercise the minds of the consumers and an agitation may be set off. Then it becomes news of wide interest.

Likewise a steep fall in prices may adversely affect the farmers and they may arrive in strength in the capital demanding the government intervene in the market to help them. It is again news.

The rise in onion prices was exploited in the 1979 parliamentary election in India.

A theft in your neighborhood may excite much interest among the locals and they may talk about it for days together. That happens because everyone who is a householder is interested in what happens to other. householders. But the interest wanes as you travel away from your neighborhood and the story may end up as a brief paragraph in the city page of the morning newspaper.

The picture would, however, alter radically if it turned out to be a big burglary or the thieves injured someone or killed a person or two, or some ingenious housebreaking device was employed by the thieves.

Thus we may say, *"New and Interesting information constitutes news."* There are other definitions but this should serve our purpose as a practical and easily understandable definition.[1] Whether it is radio or TV, or the print medium of the newspapers, the . nature of news does not alter. What is sauce for the newspaper goose is also sauce for the radio/TV gander.

Unless, of course, one or the other medium is, under rigid censorship when news values undergo radical changes and what is passed off as news ceases to be news.

Always remember that the *News is,* that is despite its seemingly plural form it is invariably singular. It must also be preceded by the definite article, the. Whenever you have to refer to information in the plural form you must say news items or news stories. Later, in this chapter, we shall see why a news item is called a story.

The news is not only new and interesting information, it also has certain ingredients which help you to distinguish a news item from one which is not.

Immediacy: The event must be fresh, almost pertaining to the last hour, if not the last minute. For the radio/TV media, the news has to be reported almost as it happens because there are hourly bulletins and the TV is also on the air for hours together during which several newscasts are part of the scheduled programmes. What is even a day old is like yesterday's leftovers, not news.

Any development brought to light after the event like the revelations on the private life of an important public figure or person of eminence can be news provided it is interesting and sheds new light on this personality. A historical or archaeological discovery can also be news specially when connected with a public controversy, like the Ayodhya dispute, in India's Uttar Pradesh (UP) state. But then it must be something which has been brought to light for the first time.

The emphasis in the news is always on *today,* and on the *last hour* in radio and TV.

Proximity: The closer you are to an event, the more newsy it is to you. Happenings in your environment would interest you much more than distant developments, however important they might he, and would, therefore, constitute news. An earthquake of severe intensity causing heavy damage to property and loss of life in distant Peru or Columbia cannot excite you as a newsman as much as one of moderate intensity in your own country, like the earthquake in the hills of UP in India in 1991, or in a neighboring country, even though less devastation might have been caused.

But if the earthquake lays a whole city waste or if Peru's independence is threatened by a big neighbor, particularly a superpower, the distance gets narrowed and the interest is heightened. Any such development in the Asian continent would, of course, be top news for you.

Proximity is not necessarily physical, it could be psychological and emotional too. People living away from their homeland sit for hours before a short wave radio. Dr a satellite TV receiver to receive news from the country of their origin and they would quickly pick up a newspaper from the country if they see one. They are emotionally close to the land of their birth, specially if they have migrated in recent years, no matter how far away they are physically.

But by and large, more distant a place the less newsy it would appear to you. All the well-intentioned talk of one world has not made the media take interest in the day-to-day developments in lands far off from their location except when the news relates to disasters and failures. (See next paragraph.).

Conflict: As in literature or films and TV serials so in news. People are less interested, you may say not interested at all, in what they perceive to be routine developments - people going to and returning from their work peacefully, being able to buy their food at reasonable prices, as and when they need it, the phenomenon of boy-meet-girl and both living happily ever after. Strikes and bandhs (work stoppages), violence and arson, wars and invasions, natural disasters and the like unfortunately interest human beings more than their opposites. An element of controversy is the spice mews men are looking for in a story.

Consequence and importance: A legislator may cross the floor of his assembly Dr parliament (and join another political party), a minister may resign, someone may die and a battle of success ion may ensue. By itself the event may seem innocuous but it could be an indication of some major developments to follow - a government may fall, a dynasty may break up and so on.

Likewise, the fact that a man is Prime Minister or President makes people interested in almost everything connected with him. That makes news because of his importance.

Drama: Finally, a news story can also have elements of drama or suspense in it. A parliamentary walkout, kidnapping, a miraculous escape, a hijack, a prime minister calling on his head of state near the midnight hour are some examples of stories with a dramatic element. The exact purpose of the prime minister disturbing the peace of the venerable head of state may not be immediately known but the story may be important all the same, even if speculation has to be avoided.

Are news persons born or made? Training is important whether or not a man has instinctive news sense, the nose for news as it is called. The feeling for news can be cultivated to a great extent, sharpened by training and perfected by practice.

A heightened sense of curiosity and keenness to know and find out about men and matters are distinct assets in anyone aspiring to journalistic laurels. But capacity to learn and readiness to work hard are essential if the news personality is to be moulded into proper shape.

I was on my way from Bombay to Singapore in November, 1967 to become the first AIR South East Asia correspondent. Hardly had the plane left the shores of India when I realised that my first story was travelling with me. As I struck up acquaintance with a senior executive of Hindustan Aircraft of Bangalore, now called Hindustan Aeronautics, I sensed that he and his colleague, a test pilot, were on an important mission and gathered that right on that airline there were two unassembled trainer aircraft. They had been made by their public sector company and India was presenting them as gifts to Malaysia and Singapore.

Naturally, this was my first story, on the morrow of my landing in Singapore. There was a bigger story when Malaysia received the gift with acclaim and enthusiasm, and Singapore which was, of course, reported but Singapore made heavy weather about arranging a ceremony and received only the papers of the aircraft in the quietude of the foreign secretary's office, which, alas, my position as a representative of the Indian official media, prevented me from reporting.

All news has to be factual. The reporter who gathers the news and the editor who brings it to the listener and viewer must check and recheck the information. All India Radio has a system of checking facts, particularly those concerning sensitive developments like communal riots and other civil disturbances, and while the report may sometimes be delayed the check on facts is generally helpful. Political developments likewise have to be reported after checking the facts with the source but there is no need to be timid and take the line of least resistance if the source behaves in a "no comment" equivocal fashion.

Voice of America, the U.S. Government radio broadcasting to the world (at home the government is barred from beaming radio or TV programmes to the people) has a system of checking major world news. At least two independent sources should be there before they broadcast a story of this nature. We in AIR had to be extremely careful about the repeated western media stories of the Chinese leader Mao Ze Dong's death as he was killed by them more than once before he actually died in 1976. When the death occurred we applied all the known factual checks before putting it out.

Generally news agencies (also called wire agencies or just agencies) make it obligatory for their reporters and editors to "source" the news, that is attribute the information to an authoritative person, a spokesman, senior officer or political figure, in a position to speak for the organisation or administration. Thus, the news media, the dailies and radio and TV stations or networks, and their readers and listeners at large know from where the information has originated. The source also takes responsibility for it.

This is a healthy practice. Unfortunately, in recent years even the news agencies have been putting out information sponsored by masked "official" sources or "circles close to the government". So, you never know whether the information is reliable or it is a story floated by interested functionaries in the government or the government itself, or an important political figure. The agencies must have the courage to refuse to be the vehicles of such news, unless the sources were ready to identify themselves and the media and the people would then be able to know who was behind it.

The story is told of an agency correspondent covering a fire and asking the fire officer, "Shall I quote you for the fire?" Since the reporter was seeing the fire himself there was no need for a source for the story on the fire. But it shows his excessive caution to "source" the story. Of course, for the cause of the fire and for the extent of damage he would have to quote the fire officer, the police and other sources. Likewise, in a political story, the party spokesman and senior leader must be quoted or indicated as the source.

Some newspapers are in the habit of carrying a story attributed to an anonymous source. They would say; "This paper was told by so-and-so (who is knowledgeable) on condition of anonymity". Very conveniently the concealed source is made to lend credibility and a few quotable quotes to the story. But it goes against the grain of the dictum, "facts are sacred." There could be occasions when the source has to be concealed but it is up to the reporter's conscience to ensure that his source (or sources) are genuine and trustworthy.

The editor who propounded the dictum "facts are sacred" also said that "comment is free"[2], But there is a place for comments, the editorial columns of a newspaper, the various comment and interpretation columns, by staffers or others, the current affairs programmes of the radio and TV and their other non- bulletin news-oriented programmes.

Unfortunately for quite some time the practice has grown for reporters to colour their copy with comments and interpretation which often reflect the views of the proprietor, the editor or the reporter himself. However, the media, including radio and TV (which have a greater responsibility than the daily newspapers), must not be squeamish. They should not allow themselves to become vehicles of propaganda for the government or influential politicians who are fond of mouthing platitudes. Also the media cannot afford to make their readers or listeners wait for the interpretation to appear in the next edition or for a commentary or discussion which could follow on the radio/TV after hours or even the next day.

A measure of interpretative reporting is thus unavoidable, even necessary at times, but the reporter must act with objectivity, fairness and balance. That there is still bias in the media cannot be denied. The western media, which control the international flow of news, are particularly guilty of racial and ethnic bias, and other bias based on the economic superiority of the countries of their origin,[3] Even among Asians there can be such bias in intra-Asian matters or bias of a nationalist kind. The hallmark of a good mediaman is his capacity to rise above such predilections and preclivities.

Every news story must tell us *who* did *what, where when* and *why.* Some writers would also add *'how'* to these five elements, while others think 'why' includes 'how'. The five W's and the H should be brought to the audience in the *lead or intra* (short for introduction) or soon after the first or first two sentences. Other details, also referred to as the *other points of the story,* can follow in the rest of the story called the *body* of the news story.

"Three persons were killed and fifteen injured in fresh incidents of communal violence in the old city of Hyderabad today".

This is a good example of all the five W's being brought into the lead sentence of the story in a natural manner. The unfortunate persons who lost their lives being the *who,* along with the fifteen injured, their being killed or injured constituting *what* of the story, the old city of Hyderabad the *where* the violence taking place *today* showing the *when* of it all and the fact of communal violence the *why.*

As you proceed further the likely cause of the riot, the law and order action taken by the authorities (like the imposition of a curfew, calling out of additional forces to control the mobs and so on), the hospitalisation of the injured, visits of a minister to the riot-hit areas and statements by the opposition parties on the incidents are some of the other points which would follow.

You would notice that the lead tells us what happened, in which the listener is primarily interested, followed by the why and how of it. We have already indicated in the lead that the place has a history of communal violence of a recent period or a remote age.

A news item is called a *story* because it is expected to be told in an interesting manner like a story and take care of all the elements that go to make up a story.

Unlike the grandmother's bedtime story, ours has to be told in the reverse order, in the shape of an *inverted pyramid that is the climax must come first.* The grandmother holds it back until the end of her story by which perhaps the child is already asleep. The listeners want *the news first,* the climax first, telling then what happened in the first instance, followed by the other points.

The reason is simple. It is human nature to expect to be told what happened first, the details being filled in later. It is like people wanting to know 'boy or girl' first, or sometimes only that. The newsman has, therefore, to reverse the order of the story.

To illustrate the point further, let us take the case of a man you have sent out to collect a cheque from a person reputed to be difficult in the matter of paying his dues. When he returns, you want to know first of all whether the cheque has been obtained or not. You would be exasperated if the errand man began telling you of his commuting woes, how he missed the 11-30 bus, how he came before the 12 noon bus along with his friend from another office on his motorbike and gave him a lift and so on. You would shout, "But first tell me if you got the cheque or not". You would perhaps then have time to listen to his commuting problem if he first came out with the outcome of his mission, the lead of the story.

Then there is the story of the manservant who went to the railway station to meet his master who was returning after a fairly long trip. Finding the servant somewhat gloomy, the master asked him: "Everything fine at home, Babu?"

"Nothing wrong, Sir. The poor dog got burnt."

"But, how?"

"When we had this fire in the house, some burning plaster fell on the dog."

"Fire? What caused the fire?"

"When your mother-in-law died we had lighted a lamp mear the body and the curtains caught fire."

"Mother dead? But I had left her in pretty good shape?"

"She died of shock when the madam ran away with the chauffeur."

Obviously the servant was a good student of psychology or a clever practitioner of it. He gave the news in driblets so as to soften the shock to his master. In his case, there was also the problem to decide the real order of the points of the story. So he began with the least disturbing part.

For a newsman, however, there is neither good news nor bad news. No news is good news may be all right in a certain context but in a news person's daily budget a good story is that which has more news appeal, whether it is good news or bad news.

The pattern of presenting news and the manner in which the story has to be told is thus broadly clear. But there is scope nay there is need, for variation in presentation of the facts of a story. We shall have occasion to go into it in detail later on.

The point to be grasped here is that the audience is interested first in who won or who lost, who has been appointed, who disappointed, who arrived, and better still who failed to arrive. The most newsy part must form your lead and must precede the other points.

Notes:

1. Compare: "As a working definition one can say that NEWS is a new piece of information about a significant and recent event that affects the listeners and is of interest to them. *Here's the NEWS,* compiled and edited by Paul De Maeseneer, Asian Books, New Delhi.

2. C.P. Scott, Editor, *Manchester Guardian* (now the *Guardian)*
3. See "India of 80's gets little more than Crisis Coverage in *'The New York Times'* by Ravi Balasubramaniam in the *Times of India,* New Delhi, November 1, 1992.

He says: "America's leading newspaper, the *New York Times,* gave India little more than "crisis coverage" through the 1980's a recent study has revealed.

Nearly 70 per cent of the news reports about India were found to be about unrest or dissent, terrorist or separatist activity, violence and killings, assassinations, crime and disaster-related events.

The random sample study conducted by this correspondent and colleagues at Northern Illinois university examined 180 issues of the newspaper over the decade. The study indicated that news values like violence, conflict and controversy dominated news coverage of the country in the years randomly selected: 1982, 1983, 1985,-1986 and 1989. An image of India that came through was one of corruption and violence."

For further reading on the broad subject of "Broadcast Journalism," see "Books For Further Reading" at the end of this book.

EXERCISES:

1. Attempt your own definition of news and discuss it.
2. Are the media showing enough awareness of "Fact are Sacred"? Discuss.
3. Make a list of recent radio/TV reports or reports in the daily press which cannot strictly be called "news".

Chapter II

THE SPOKEN WORD

Radio is a medium which you have to hear, television has both to be heard and seen and the printed medium only to be read. In the newscasts of the visual medium, the words spoken by the news presenter as much as the visuals, the captions, and the personality of the presenter, to an extent, form part of the total newscast.

Words, however, have a significant, if not a major, role to play.

Thus, both in radio and TV, the spoken word is of great consequence, the news is brought to you in the spoken word in its entirety by a faceless news reader in one case and by a presenter, appearing on the screen, in his or her words, aided by visuals, in the other.

The spoken word idiom is basically different from the one employed by the print medium. A newspaper is taken in by the eye, most often in driblets, in small doses. Only a small number of readers go through their daily paper at one go. Most of us scan the front page headlines, the sports or commercial page, according to our taste, glance through the other pages and read some news stories, a column and an editorial at leisure.

For a considerable section of readers, however the paper is done with for the day after they have gone through the first process i.e. they read the front page headlines and a story or two, see the commercial and/or sports page, run their eyes over the other pages and put it aside.

In any case, while reading the paper you can read the same thing twice or thrice. If a word, phrase or sentence is difficult to understand, you can also turn to the dictionary or consult someone else if you are not able to grasp the meaning of what you read.

Not so with the radio or TV bulletin. It has to be absorbed as it goes on the air. If you stumble on something unintelligible to you or your mind is made to think of what the Radio/TV says amounts to, you may miss the rest of the bulletin or much of it. In other words, the electronic media editor has to ensure that he holds the attention of the listener or viewer all the time.

Neither the radio audience is a captive one nor are the TV viewers without an alternative. Both media have cut across national frontiers and if the audience is dissatisfied with the bulletins from a particular station or network it can tune into some other. Both the contents and their presentation have to be such as would hold the attention of the audience. But above all, the spoken word nature of the two media must be fully reflected in the script.

What you *write* for the radio or TV has to be *heard* by the audience. When you write news for the radio and TV the most essential point to borne in mind is that you are **not writing to be read,** taken in by the eye as in the case of the print medium, but to be **heard.** This calls for the use of words, language and sentences which we employ in conversation, in day-to-day circumstances, in our interpersonal contacts. When the listener or viewer hears your bulletin it should be easy on his ears. It should be easily intelligible to him by virtue of the familiar words and coversational style used.

For example, when we speak to one another we place the figure or amount of money first and the currency afterwards. We say: "This pen cost me **fifty rupees**" not rupees fifty, or Rs. 50, which is the form used in the printed medium. Since the radio and TV bulletins are *read out to be heard,* the style followed therein must be akin to the spoken word. We have to say in our bulletins, "the bridge will cost, or will be built at a cost of, seventy million rupees," not Rs. 70 million.

Likewise, we refer to the time of any past event or forthcoming event or happening with reference to *today.* We tell each other: "Let us meet tomorrow to finalise this deal." we do not say, "Let us meet on January 15" if it happens to be January 14 when the conversation takes place. As far as possible we avoid mentioning the date if it is close to "today". The Prime Minister will leave Delhi for Tokyo *tomorrow,* not January 15. Obviously, we cause the listener much less strain by mentioning not the date, because if we did he will have to figure it out when January 15 would fall.

Similarly, what happened on January 13 would be referred to as "yesterday" and February has to be referred to "next month", 1994 as "next year" and 1992 as "last year".

The reason for doing so is that is how we speak to others in our conversation while the print medium would refer to the events in terms of January 15, or 13, of 1994 or 1992, even if the story were to say: "The Prime Minister will leave Delhi for Tokyo *tomorrow, January* 15". If you were to employ the print form in a radio or TV bulletin the audience would be compelled to think about the date and month; when is January 15, oh, today it is January 14, so tomorrow will be January 15. In the process part of your bulletin is lost on the listener.

The aim is to ensure uninterrupted absorption of your message, the news bulletin transmitted on radio or TV, and avoid putting undue strain on the audience. The language has to be simple, sentences short and words familiar, and the time frame has to be borne in mind.

There is no halfway house. Either the listener understands you while the newscast is on the air or he does not get you at all. There is no going back and forth as while reading a newspaper. If you must use a newfangled expression you must explain it in the bulletin itself, until the word becomes largely integrated with the day-to-day language of the people.

Figures have to be read out clearly in stories with an economic flavour. Names occurring for the first time or otherwise have to be distinctly and correctly pronounced. The TV must always use the facility of captions when an unfamiliar name is the focal point of the story, like a Nobel prize award or an important appointment, so that the viewer grasps what you are talking about:

"Mr. Rip Van Winkle has been appointed *Vigilance Commissioner":*

Both the name and designation must be read clearly so as to make an impression on the viewer. Often you succeed in catching only "has been appointed" and possibly "Commissioner", thus missing the main news.

The news agencies, which are an important source of news to you, write in a style which suits the print medium. These stories are also long and sometimes long- winding. These have to be rewritten, radio-written or TV-written, before you include them in your bulletin.

The same goes for official handouts or statements of political parties which employ a heavy jargon. Official handouts, based as they are on government files, are written in officialese although the press relations staff who hand them out are supposed to put them in journalistic language or journalese. These have also to be rewritten by you.

These may appear to be elementary precautions but all the same they are important. They are liable to be ignored or overlooked, as, indeed, they often are.

In schools and colleges, we seem to tell the young boys and girls *Write to impress, not to communicate,* to display scholarship not to aim at being understood. With the result that often the newspaper reporter or writer flaunts a difficult style, not easy to comprehend.

Long-widening sentences, difficult and unfamiliar words, clauses within clauses, and several points of information crammed into a single sentence become role models. The young people who find this style in practice in the leading dailies feel inclined to emulate it. All this makes the task of unlearning the over-elaborate style and learning the simple one of short sentences and familiar day-to-day words essential and urgent if you have to make a good radio/TV journalist.

Here is a not untypical sample, from the *Statesman* of New Delhi dated October 26, 1992, of the style of long sentences:

"Despite initial attempts from certain quarters to stonewall its effective functioning, the Joint Parliamentary Committee, inquiring into the multi-crore rupee security scam, in its 80 days of functioning, has succeeded in projecting itself as a serious fact finding body determined to get to the bottom of the fraud.

At the end of the first round of questioning of major players involved in the scam, the story that has unfolded before the JPC is one of total disregard for rules and regulations, wanton flouting of established guidelines and repeated abuse of all regulatory mechanism to monitor the securities transactions, with the list of crimes committed ranging from forgery to outright favoritism.

While the JPC is still in the process of sifting through the massive amount of evidence that has been collected, it would be worthwhile to look at the work done, the nature of evidence that has been collected against the prominent players and the line of defence that they have advanced."

There are more of the same paragraph-long sentences, each sentence running into 50 words or more on the average. The middle para quoted above has words.

Long sentences can be split while rewriting them for broadcast. Wherever you see the conjunction "and", you should use your blue pencil and start a new sentence.

For example, the following is really two sentences:

"The lower house of Parliament today observed a two minute silence in honour of two of its sitting members who died over the weekend and later passed a bill to create a national commission to protect the rights of women." This should have been written as: "The lower house of Parliament today passed a bill to create a national commission for women. Earlier it mourned the death of two of its sitting members over the weekend by observing two minutes silence."

If long and difficult sentences are read over the radio or TV at high speed (some TV presenters erroneously think they have to speed up) much of it is sure to go over the heads of the listeners. For us the difficult is ugly, not beautiful, and so is the long sentence.

An essential principle of communication is that the message, in this case the news stories, and the bulletin of which it is made, must be intelligible to the audience, the radio/TV listeners and viewers. The message is meant for the audience not for the satisfaction of the communicator, the bulletin editor. He has to realise that he must make his message as simple and easy to grasp as he can. He must never fall prey to the false notion that things have to be made difficult before you place them before your audience.

He would greatly facilitate his task if he remembers that what he is *writing* is to be *read out*. The story must sound easy, conversational and intelligible to the listener who may not be highly educated.

Just as the editor has to say *"five million rupees" not "Rupees five million",* because the former is the spoken word form, he has also to avoid usages like "former" and "latter". The reason is that in radio/TV there is nothing that is above and nothing which is below, as there is in the printed newspaper medium. You have to explain what you mean without resorting to this device.

There is also **no dateline** for the radio/I'V bulletins. The date and place have to be woven into the story without making it too cumbersome either.

"The Malaysian Prime Minister, Dr Mahatir Mohammad, arrived in Delhi today to begin a four day official visit to India."

In a newspaper you would say: *"New Delhi: January* 15 - Dr Mahatir Mohammad, Prime Minister of Malaysia, arrived *here today* at the start of an official visit to India." (Delhi and New Delhi are for all practical purposes one and the same).

Incidentally, both sentences above take care of all the W's.

Now we come to a very important point concerning the spoken word media, namely, the **need for brevity.** The radio/TV editor has to cut the coat to suit the limited cloth available to him. A standard radio bulletin is of ten minutes. There are several smaller ones, like the hourly bulletins which; are generally of five minutes duration, and there are a few of fifteen minute duration, like the evening 2045 and 2100 hours Hindi and English bulletins of AIR. Read at a fairly brisk pace, but not very fast, the ten minute bulletin can accommodate not more than 1,400 words. Of this some 100 words will be consumed by the four headlines at the beginning and the news summary at the end.

The body of the bulletin is thus reduced to 1,300 words in which you must convey the gist of all that has happened in the period since the last bulletin earlier that morning, if yours is an evening bulletin, or the pervious evening, if you are doing a morning bulletin. The evening bulletin editor must tell his listener what all has happened during the day. And since most important home stories break during the day his task is all the more formidable.

Just 1,400 words strictly speaking 1,300 words only, are much less than what a standard newspaper column would have. And the newspapers have many, many columns. Each radio item must, therefore, be reduced to its barest essentials, pruning it of all points that can be dispensed with. Only then can you find the time to give your listeners a wide spectrum of news and thus lend variety to your bulletin and also make it comprehensive. The bulletin must cover major home stories as well as important world news and news of the neighbouring countries as well as interesting home and world sports.

At that rate you can hope to include about twelve, sometimes fourteen, different items in your ten-minute newscast. *The average length of a radio story being 80- 100 words* a total of 12 to 14 items is thus a reasonable number to aim at. Of course, some of the items could be smaller, and these could be disposed of in 50 words or less while some items would, of necessity, be longer than 100 words. Your lead story about a major national development could, for example, be of that length.

The standard TV newscasts vary from 15-20 minutes, to half an hour, and sometimes longer. The longer duration is accounted for by the presence of visuals which are easy on the eye and make the bulletin more interesting. The variety of 'voice over' dispatches from correspondents or other sources which it is easier for TV to bring to the viewers than a radio bulletin can also facilitate the watching by the viewers. Normally the ear which is the organ addressed by the radio broadcast is not capable of taking in more at a time. A fifteen minute news broadcast is the outside limit.

In other words, the radio/TV editor has to exercise the utmost economy, cutting out all unessential and several of the less essential points too. He has to reach the core of the news and dispense with all the sidelights and embellishments and many of the details. Ours are not the media for detail.

The TV medium, and to a certain extent the radio too, can, however, bring to the audience a variety of view-points, a range of developments and different aspects of the story, through programmes other than the bulletin. Such programmes may include a discussion, a mix of interviews and comments, interpretative commentaries, newsreels and field despatches.

Intelligently presented, with fairness and balance, such programmes would not only be highly satisfying to the audience but theat would also obviate to a great extent the need for the more interested among the audience to gather too many details from the print medium.

The radio/TV editor has to learn the technique of leaving out many points of a story, just as in life you have to practice the art of saying 'no' both in your day-to-day interaction and at work in the office or in your business.

Details are for the print medium, not for us in the broadcast media, Radio/TV stories have to be measured in units of ten-50 words, 100 words, 150 words - not of hundreds as in the print medium. The interested listener gathers more details and fills the gaps in his information by picking them up from next day's paper. The print medium is also the medium of record. For us brevity is the soul of news, as much as of wit.

The spoken word nature imposes a few other requirements on us so that the end product - our news bulletin - becomes acceptable to the audience. What may pass muster in the print medium will sound jarring on the ears of the listener. For example, if you repeat a word or phrase in a story or even in a story following the first you will make the listener feel unhappy. Substitutes have to be found for words which may occur again and again, as far as possible.

The name and designation of a personality in the news need not be repeated every time. For well known people like the President or Prime Minister it is enough to begin by their designation. The name can follow in the second or third sentence. In the newspapers, in every story the name and designation is repeated as they are treated as independent items. In the radio/TV bulletin the connected stories have to be linked, integrated into a whole. The name and designation cannot be used in each part of the item.

Initials and personal names can be dispensed with in most cases, except when an appointment is announced. It is enough to say “the Prime Minister, Mr Narasimha Rao”, and not, “the Prime Minister Mr P.V. Narasimha Rao”. “Home Minister Chavan” “should be preferred to” the Home Minister; Mr S.B. Chavan.”

In doing this, we not only avoid repeating names and avoid using words which are unnecessary, we also practice economy of words which is one of our principal concerns. If in a ten-minute bulletin you economise on such names and designations to the extent of 40-50 words, you can accommodate an additional news item. In the process we are also making it easier for the listener to take in our bulletin.

The neglect of this guideline often leads broadcasters into serious errors. In a TV dispatch, a correspondent covering the Prime Minister's visit to a foreign country was found to be saying in every sentence "the Prime Minister, Mr P .V. Narasimha Rao" and thereby he caused the audience to feel uneasy. He also lost nearly a tenth of the time at his disposal by uttering the name and designation of the head of government a dozen times.

There is an interesting parallel on the importance of economy of words. In ancient India, the writers of standard works on different aspects of science, philosophy, grammar and other serious subjects used to compose aphorisms *sutras,* which would be easy for the students to make by heart. The commentary on each aphorism would elaborate the point or points in it. Such was the urge of the writers of these works, the *sutrakaras,* to effect economy of words that there was a saying:

"the writers of the aphorisms celebrate the saving of a single syllable like the birth of a son."

Notes:

1. The following interesting and instructive incident sheds light on the spoken word style:

   At that meeting the veteran CBS correspondent (Charles Collingwood) talked about his first association with Ed Murrow (veteran broadcaster). It was at the beginning of World War II and Collingwood, who had been working for the United Press, had just been hired by Murrow in London. He said: "I was fascinated by the difference between writing for this new, bumptious medium of radio and conforming to the canons of wire service journalism. So even before I went on the CBS payroll I went around to Murrow's office and pored over his script files looking for clues. It seems to me I said, *that your formula is to write short, vivid declarative sentences, using dependent clauses only to vary the pace or for ornamentation.* Ed Murrow looked at me in some surprise and said, 'Oh, is that what I do. I had never thought about it.'

From *Writing News for Broadcast,* Edward Bliss, Jr and John M. Patterson, Columbia University Press, New York, page 2 (Emphasis added)

2. The same book gives a sample of Ed Murrow's radio writings: "Christmas Day began in London nearly an hour ago. The church bells did not ring at midnight. When they ring again it will be to announce invasion. And if they ring, the British are ready."

EXERCISES:

1. Render for the spoken word media the three paragraphs quoted in the chapter from the *Statesman* newspaper.
2. Explain with examples, how the spoken word idiom is different from the printed medium language.
3. Pick up a story from a leading daily of your city/region and rewrite it as a Radio/TV news item.

Chapter III

NEWSWRITING - SOME GUIDELINES

The budding Radio/TV journalist, as well as his practicing counterpart, can never afford to lose sight of the fact that he is writing for the spoken word medium. He is writing for being *read aloud*. What he is writing is to be ***read out* to be *heard*.** He is writing for the ear, not for the eye.

It is essential, therefore, that

- your sentences should be short.
- you should use simple and familiar words in preference to difficult and less known words.
- your should prefer the active form of speech to the passive.
- you have to go to the heart of the story, cut out all unessential and less essential points. Find the hard core of the news.
- you should remember the average length of a news story for radio/TV is 80-100 words, although a few stories could be longer and several others even shorter.
- in your media the news must necessarily be presented in a nutshell.
- you must remember that the news agencies (a major source of news for you) work basically for the print medium, their newspaper clients, and write the kind of language they use. Their stories go to the length that

the print media require. Brevity is not the soul of their wit, but for you it is your tool of trade.

- you remember that connected radio/TV stories have to be rewritten as integrated news items.
- you should note that your frame of reference is different. So, there is no above or below, no former and latter, for radio/TV.
- You should use variation to reduce monotony and impart interest to your story.
- The sentences of your stories must be complete, even for the headlines of the bulletin also called the main points. Each sentence should be linked to the previous and the following ones, as far as possible.

When a story, unconnected with the previous story, is introduced in the bulletin (as you may have too often) use devices to help you bring in the new story. Like *"At* the United Nations." *"IN* Bombay today", *"MEANWHILE* in New Delhi", which signify that you are now on to something different. You have to introduce a new story to help the listener grasp that something else is being talked about. As far as possible, some effort must be made to demarcate a story from another unless several stories form part of a major development and are thus connected with one another.

This underlines the point that stories drafted individually as radio/TV items, out of the agency copy or your reporter's copy or handouts tendered at your desk must be suitably redrafted or touched up while they are being included in your bulletin.

Death should be generally reported as "The death occurred in New Delhi (or whatever the place) today of Mr ... " If you merely said "Mr ... died in New Delhi today" the listener hearing the name might think this is yet another homily from that junior or senior VIP and switch off his mind from your story. He might miss the death part of the story altogether. But if you start with death the listener sits up and takes notice.

Similarly we can also resort to this device to report a resignation or an appointment. "The resignation has been announced or reported of Mr ... " or "the appointment has been announced of Mr ... as ... " There can be no hard and fast rule about such practices but the important point to remember is that you have to attract and hold the listener's attention. Devices which help you to achieve this objective have to be employed.

Let us look at a couple of typical long sentences in the daily press and see how we can rewrite them in a style suitable for radio/TV. Here is an example from the *Times of India,* Delhi of November 5, 1992.

"In fairness, however, it must be added that the factors contributing also to an unprecedented warmth between New Delhi and Washington, in recent months, as highlighted by growing contacts in the military field, will retain their relevance because of the underlying geopolitical realities, chief among them being India's proximity to the Gulf".

This 52-word sentence constituting an entire paragraph can be redrafted as follows:

"However, the factors which have contributed to the recent warmth in Delhi's ties with Washington, not seen before, will retain their relevance. This is chiefly because of India's nearness to the Gulf and other geopolitical reasons. Growing military contacts have marked this relationship".

We have achieved a little economy of words and a distinct simplification of ideas apart from words. The unduly long and complex sentence has been made easy for the reader or listener to follow, without sacrificing any point or even the key words.

Here is another example of long-windedness and too many ideas packed in a single sentence taken from the *Indian Express,* Delhi, of the same date:

"Braving snow in some places and long lines almost everywhere, a record turnout of about almost 100 million voters, reversing the 32-year decline in voter participation, swept the Democratic party leader into the White House on Wednesday, ousting George Bush from the post, he hoped to retain for the second term running."

This can be rewritten as:

"The record turnout of about 100 million voters swept Democratic leader Bill Clinton to power ending President Bush's dream of a second term. In some places the voters braved snow and everywhere they encountered long lines."

There is in our version a significant saving of words. This is important because, as we have seen, words saved make room for one or two more stories in our bulletin apart from making the language suitable for broadcast. As in the first case, we have not omitted any important point or changed many of the words in the original.

But our aim is to simplify the language and present the ideas or points as intelligibly as possible. The following version of the first example noted above attempts to do that:

"But the warmth seen recently in Indo-American relations may continue. India's nearness to the Gulf and other geopolitical factors will ensure that. Growing military contacts are an example of these warm ties."

Not only the economy of words is noteworthy but also the ideas have achieved clarity. The language is quite suitable for broadcast. Except "geopolitical" there is not one word which is unfamiliar to the average listener.

Writing for the broadcast media is primarily part of good writing. Those aiming to write well even in the print media cannot do better than emulate this style, as many journalists and writers are doing these days.

Once you grasp the underlying principle and put it into practice it will become part of your style. Anything you write will thus fall in place and will be suitable for radio/TV, apart from anything else.

Studies have been made on the length of sentences according to which 17 words per sentence on an average are considered a reasonable limit. Some sentences, according to these studies, could have more words but some others could have fewer making a good balanced passage. It is not necessary for you to count the words in a sentence. What matters is making a habit of keeping your sentences short. If you cannot. curtail the length of a particular sentence you should aim at having other sentences short so that you achieve an overall effect of having only short sentences in your copy, making it easy for the listener to follow you.

You should studiously avoid packing too many ideas or points in a single sentence as in the examples we have quoted above.

It is the tendency of saying so many things at the same time in a single sentence that makes us fall into the error of writing lengthy, almost unwieldy sentences. For the radio listener who is not face to face with the newsreader it is a great disadvantage to be plied with such long sentences. Even for a TV viewer the bombardment simply distracts his mind from the story. While the accompanying visuals hold his attention the lengthy sentences are almost lost on him.

Economy has to be our watchword and you need not say: "The President of the United States, Mr Bill Clinton" It would suffice to say "American President Bill Clinton", "President Clinton of the United States" or just "President Clinton", since such figures are well known to most listeners.

"The President of the Republic of Mongolia" should be rendered as "the Mongolian President". Only republics have Presidents. So it is redundant to refer to both the republic and its President in the same breath. Likewise Home Minister Chavan would be sufficient for our purpose, not the Home Minister, Mr. S. B. Chavan. The latter is more alien to the spoken word style and the former helps us save a few words. Initials and first names are generally dropped in our bulletins except when they are relevant.

Avoiding repetition and introducing variation is another device by which you serve the *twin objective of economy of words and using the spoken word idiom.*

In the parliamentary system the Prime Minister is always making news. He is the most important national figure. It is not, therefore, necessary to mention him both by name and designation. Also, since there could be more than one reference to him in your bulletin you could safely avoid the name in a minor item.

For example, the name and designation may be alternately used, along with a pronoun in between, in a major story like his intervention in a parliamentary discussion. In a subsequent story you may simply say:

"The Prime Minister called on President Shanker Dayal Sharma at Rashtrapati Bhavan in New Delhi this afternoon. An official spokesman described the meeting as routine."

The rule on avoiding repetitions applies to other personalities and situations as well. Suppose the story is about people being rescued from under the debris of a house which has collapsed. You do not have to use the obvious expression "heart-rending" cries every time you refer to the people shouting to be rescued or the relatives and friends standing there and watching the rescue work. You have to look for variants - "made repeated pleas" for rescue. "the relatives and friends of the trapped people appealed to the firemen to speed up the rescue operations."

Avoid cliches, even journalistic cliches like "the police found nothing *incriminating*". You can simply say: "The police searched the premises but found no proof of any crime."

Another way of introducing variation is using a different form of lead. Some stories may not yield much by way of hot news but may be otherwise interesting like an international gathering of government representatives. In such cases the lead could well be:

"Delegates from the seven South Asian nations met in Delhi today to discuss ways to educate the people in preventing AIDS." *Or* "in Delhi today, delegates from the seven SAARC countries ... "

Let us suppose the following handout is made available to you:

"New Delhi, November 3, 1992: The Secretary of the Department of Science and Technology, Dr Rama Rao, has called upon the representatives of SAARC countries to identify specific areas in science and technology for cooperation and optimum utilisation of resources for the mutual benefit of the member countries. Inaugurating the 10th meeting of SAARC Technical Committee on Science and Technology here today, Dr. Rama Rao stressed the need for application of Science & Technology for national development in view of the limited natural resources available in the region. It is in the interest of the SAARC countries that the representatives should work out a coordinated approach for the optimum utilization of available resources for the ultimate benefit of the people in the region. He said during the deliberation key institutes and establishments should be identified so that the young scientists of the SAARC countries could have access to the data bases available in different fields. The young

scientists should also be encouraged to visit the scientific establishments in the SAARC countries for a better understanding and exchange of views and information.

The meeting was presided over by Dr. J. Dhar, Advisor, Department of Science & Technology and Chairman, SAARC Technical Committee on Science & Technology.

Delegates from Bangladesh, Bhutan, India, Maldives, - Nepal, Pakistan and Sri Lanka are attending the three- day deliberations held in New Delhi for second time. During the deliberation the SAARC Technical Committee will review the activities and examine the recommendations of the Seminars/Workshops held since the last meeting. They will also examine and approve programmes which can be implemented in the near future.

Since you are concerned with hard news you may feel this certainly is not hard news. But all networks have to cope with such stories and we can still make an interesting story out of it like this:

"Delegates from seven South Asian nations began a three day meeting in Delhi today to achieve greater cooperation in the field of Science and Technology. The seven countries are Bangladesh, Bhutan, the Maldives, Nepal, Pakistan and Sri Lanka, besides the host nation India. They are the members of SAARC, South Asian Association for Regional Cooperation. The Secretary of the Department of Science and Technology Dr. Rama Rao, opened the meeting. In his address, Dr. Rama Rao stressed the need for the optimum use of resources and urged the delegates to identify areas of cooperation."

If, by a coincidence, there is another SAARC meeting the same day, say on checking the spread of AIDS, you need not repeat details like the names of the SAARC nations. You can come straight to the point thus:

"In Colombo, capital of Sri Lanka, the question of

checking the spread of AIDS was discussed today by health specialists from the SAARC nations."

This can be followed by other relevant details. The two stories have to go one after the other in your bulletin. Interesting conclusions reached by the delegates of the two conferences with positive action plans, if any, could be reported on the final day of the get-together.

The idea is to extract a little bit of newsy information from dull official handouts and present them in an interesting and easy style.

Words have to be chosen carefully so as to avoid difficult and unfamiliar words as far as possible. Some words have simple substitutes which should form part of your radio/TV vocabulary. For example, you should always say *end,* not *conclude,* "The talks (not negotiations) ended on a hopeful (not optimistic) note."

You should compile, during your work, an exhaustive list of words to be avoided and the simpler alternatives which you can employ. As we have stressed before, it is important to get into the habit of using the simpler variants which should come automatically and effortlessly to you as you do your news writing.

The following is only an illustrative list:

To *end*	not	to *conclude*
To *set up*	not	to *establish / constitute*
To *carry out*	not	to *implement*
To *begin*	not	to *commence*
To *open*	not	to *inaugurate*
opening	not	*inauguration*
About	not	*in regard to, as regards apropos of*
achieve	not	*in order to achieve*

Delay	not	*procrastination*
To *make necessary*	not	to *necessitate*
Bad weather	not	*inclement* weather
That which reminds	not	*reminiscent*
Memories	not	*reminiscences*

Of course, some words have a special context. In the United States, they say "the inauguration of the new president" and you cannot substitute "Inauguration" here by "opening." Names likewise have to be rendered correctly; like "*The Reminiscences of John* F. *Kennedy,*" if you are referring to a book of such a name.

The essential point to be noted is that simple and easy words, words of day-to-day use should be preferred to difficult and unfamiliar words. You have to simplify your language and effect economy of words. Thereby you make the listener's task easy and this helps you in holding his attention.

Some other useful points may also be noted here. Figures of money or other amounts must be rounded off to a convenient figure. If the World Bank has sanctioned a loan of $500,375,250 million you have to say the World Bank has sanctioned India a loan of slightly over 500 million dollars.

If the Government has imposed new taxes of Rs. 535,875,425 you can say, new taxes worth nearly 536 million rupees have been levied.

Where, however, the exact figure is crucial or relevant, like the score in cricket matches, you have to render it as such. There again, after giving the scores of the rival teams and other interesting details you can say "the other notable contributions came from ... "

The general rule that too many details are not for us is relevant here. The interested listener is sure to gather more information from the next day's newspaper. Also, too many details strain the listener's hearing and the average listener who is your target may not also be interested in them. It is bad enough, insofar as he is concerned, that heavy taxes have been imposed. Do you have to put another load on his mind and give him a whole lot of figures?

EXERCISES:

1. Why is it important to keep down the length of stories in a radio bulletin?
2. Write on the importance of variation in newswriting, with examples.
3. Compile a list of words to be avoided in radio bulletins with their simpler equivalents.

Chapter IV

WRITING A STORY

We have discussed how a news story is different from the grandmother's entertaining bedtime story, what constitutes news, the essentials of the spoken word medium and the basic guidelines for writing radio/TV news. We have now reached a stage when we have a plunge into water and start our swimming practice, the practice of writing news for the electronic media.

There is an elaborate system of news gathering and reporting which finally brings the news copy to your desk. All copy is however, not necessarily news for your audience and all of it may not even be news in the general sense. You have, therefore, to apply rigid tests before you choose an item for writing for your bulletin.

First, let us see the main sources of news for any broadcast journalist. They are:

1. National and international news agencies;
2. The organization's own reporters including parttimers and stringers; and
3. News bulletins broadcast by foreign radio stations monitored by your organization.

In addition, handouts tendered at your desk by official publicity organizations of the government and by political parties, major trade unions and others can be a source. For TV the visual materials supplied by international visual agencies and those received on an exchange basis from foreign national networks cooperating with yours have to be taken into account as a source.

The news agencies have elaborate news gathering arrangements and they are also the first to be contacted by people who may have information to be handed out. They are operating round the clock. In India, the two national agencies, Press Trust of India and the United News of India, PTI and UNI, have links with international news agencies like Reuters, AP, Associated Press (of America), AFP, Agence France Presse, and others, including some foreign national agencies.

So their teleprinters, tickers or wire, as they are differently called, bring you news from home and abroad round the clock. In some countries the international news agencies are allowed to "creed" or transmit their copy direct to radio/TV or newspapers. There the Radio/TV organizations have both the home and international agencies at their disposal.

The agency copy*, as we have seen, is written basically for the print media and its length is also fit for the newspapers. You have to transform it into the spoken word idiom and cut it to its bones, keeping the average length of 80-100 words in mind.

However, there is a distinct advantage also. The agency copy is usually well edited by the agency's desk and generally speaking it also carries the lead in the opening sentence or paragraph. The points are well brought out and arranged coherently. As compared with handouts and statements presented to you at the desk, there is thus a substantial help in the agency copy. There is no reason why you should not avail of a well edited story as a source.

---

*Any news material, particularly a finished story, is called in the newsman's jargon "Copy" like agency copy, reporter's copy, Pool copy. It is used in the singular and without any article. Also used in advertising and generally in printing.

Your reporter's copy is expected to be as good as any story drafted by you, that is, written in the radio style, brief and to the point. He is a trained broadcast journalist like you and should know not only the essentials of the medium and the basics of news but also the requirements of different bulletins and the time schedule of the news broadcasts. His copy should be as finished as yours, ready to be taken to the studio direct if the bulletin is about to go on the air or is already on the air.

But reporters function under several constraints, have to rush from assignment to assignment and may for that or other reason not be able to give you a clean radioworthy item. Some reporters may be very good as news gatherers but because they have not had enough time to master the medium or otherwise may not be able to put things together in a nutshell.

This calls for the reporter's copy to be scrutinized and edited at your desk carefully. If any significant detail has been omitted you have to ensure that the lacuna is made good. A reporter could forget to mention the name of the city or town, the *where* of the story, in describing an event. You have to check up and supply the name.

The news agencies, as we have seen, write their copy with their newspaper clients in mind, although in the United States there has been a practice for the wire agencies to give a complete newscast to the smaller radio stations. The agencies also write their copy in the elaborate newspaper style. That means you have to rewrite the stories received from the agencies to suit the requirements of the spoken word and of brevity.

You have to ensure that the lead is the right one. Sometimes the agency desk may also err and play up a less important point.

Monitoring reports are generally well-written ready-made stories, cut and dry, to suit your needs. They are presumed to have been radiowritten by the same kind of professional people as you. But you have to ensure that while you pick up the items of hard news you steer clear off some of the stories written from a nationalist or partisan point of view. This caution of separating news from propaganda also applies to the stories carried by some of the foreign news agencies which cannot shed their national or other bias.

Official and party handouts are nowhere near a news item in presentation, although they may contain elements of news. You have to rewrite them thoroughly and transform them completely into radio stories. They have to be cleansed of their official or political jargon Once the material is in your hands, you have to subject it to the following process:

1. Decide whether it constitutes a news item for your medium and the audience you have in view. If the material fails to pass that test all you have to do is to put it in the 'Rejects' tray. In every organization this task is performed by a senior editorial person but even a beginer should be able to determine what is usable and what must be rejected.
2. Find the lead or intro of the story.
3. Decide the approximate number of words you will give to the story; and
4. Select the other points of the story you would like to include in your item and in what order.

We have already seen before what is involved in the process of selection of rejection of items, also called 'copy tasting.' The first examination is, of course, from the point of view of what really constitutes news. The second test is whether it is of relevance to your audiences. Every item may not be relevant to all your audiences and, therefore, all your bulletins, but it may have some interest for a particular bulletin.

In India there are many linguistic and ethnic groups and many bulletins to meet their requirements are originated by AIR.

As for the lead, the agency copy or your reporter's copy or the monitoring reports may have led the story with the right point. There is no earthly reason why you should not adopt that lead just as there is no reason why you should not be ready to alter the lead if you are convinced that the copy in front of you has not followed the proper lead. Sometimes the lead may have to be altered to suit the interest of the target audience.

For example, you may lead a story on the liberal economic policies of the government by the new measures aimed at easing bureaucratic controls. This may be good enough for the general bulletins in English and Hindi addressed to a larger national audience. But for sectional bulletins, say for the listener in Assam, you must highlight any special points of interest to that state, like a major industrial project to be located in that state which may form part of the new measures.

Brevity is our motto and the average word length of 80-100 words has thus to be rigidly observed, with exceptions in case of a couple of major stories. This would, of course, be set off by a number of smaller items. As you determine the length of a story the points you would like to include would automatically be selected alongside and you would have a mental picture of the order in which they would figure in your story.

Often it is convenient to underline or sideline the points in the original which you wish to include and mark the portion you have selected for the lead. This may be helpful when you have to weed through a large number of copy matter and you are liable to lose track of the story you are to handle after the bunch of messages awaiting your attention is disposed of.

Also, while covering a press conference or briefing you can underline in your notes the point you would like to lead with and the other points selected for inclusion in the story. It is possible that when you sit down to type out a story you may finally drop a point here and pick up another point there. But if you have already prepared yourself mentally by underlining or sidelining the points to be included, you can save a lot of time and be able to rush your story for the next available bulletin.

Now let us take up a few news items for writing them up as stories for broadcast. First, we may deal with agency copy and stories published in the daily press, which are finished material from which several of our news items are drafted.

"The European Community announced early on Sunday morning that the Spanish peseta and the Portuguese escudo had been devalued by 6% within the EC's exchange rate mechanism, reports Reuters.

After more than 10 hours of talks, the committee issued a statement which made no mention of any other changes in exchange rates. It also made no references to German interest rates.

The statement said Spain would immediately lift special measures on some foreign exchange transactions which it imposed after the last bout of currency turmoil in September.

The Spanish peseta was devalued by 5% during that crisis on September 17.

The statement said Spain and Portugal "will implement strictly all the measures necessary to ensure. that the objectives of there convergence programmes are achieved".

It added that Spain would give "highest priority" to meeting the budgetary targets and implementing the structural measures laid down in its convergence programme.

The Bundesbank President, Mr. Helmut Schlesinger, said on Friday that Central Bank's room for manoeuver on interest rates was limited in both directions.

So any request at the monetary committee meeting for. action on German interest rates' as part of a realignment package is likely to meet resistance from the German representatives.

Another potential problem at the meeting could be the Irish pound, which was under pressure on Friday, forcing Central Bank intervention to support it.

But Ireland is in the midst of general election campaign that could make the Government reluctant to agree to a devaluation."

Obviously, the story is a news item worthy of our attention. It cannot be rejected since our listeners, we presume, would be interested in the devaluation of some European currencies and the fate of some others which is hanging in the balance.

Coming to the selection of the LEAD, we find that the agency has rightly led with the devaluation of the currencies of two countries. But the lead sentence is much longer than required for the electronic media. So there is clearly a need for redrafting the lead sentence.

Among the points which we should include in our story, other than the lead sentence, are: no other European currency affected, no mention of change in the German lending rate and Ireland not being asked to devalue.

As to the number of words, we can safely decide that around 100 words should be a good limit.

The following ratio item emerges from our discussion above:

"The Spanish and Portuguese currencies have been devalued by six per cent. This decision was announced early this morning by the monetary committee of the European Community after a prolonged session in Brussels. The devaluation is within the exchange rate mechanism of the community.

No other European currency is affected by today's decision. The Irish currency has been under pressure but since the country is in the midst of an election campaign its devaluation was not considered. There was also no mention of any change in the bank lending rate in Germany although suggestions for a change have been made in and outside Germany."

A little background which was implicit in the story has been added in the last sentence.

You can add a little variety by naming the currencies ... peseta, escudo, mark, pound. The study can be headlined in the national bulletins and those meant for foreign audience ... "Currencies have been devalued in Spain and Portugal."

Now let us take up an Indian item, again as published in an English daily:

"The Government today denied that its statements regarding Pakistan's support to terrorists and India's desire to improve relations with that country had created a "credibility gap" in international circles.

The minister of state for external affairs, Mr. Eduardo Faleiro, told Syed Shahabuddin (Janata Dal) during question hour in the Lok Sabha that there was no conflict between the statements. While India was committed to a dialogue to improve relations with Pakistan, there was no question of any compromise on fundamental issues.

Asserting that there was no credibility gap as alleged by the JD member, Mr. Faleiro claimed that many countries, including the US and Britain, were now convinced of Pakistan's support to terrorism. Some of them even appeared to be in favour of declaring Pakistan a terrorist state. He told Syed Shahabuddin that he could provide documentary proof relating to Pakistan's involvement in terrorism in Kashmir from May 1988 to July this year and he could pass it on to those who have any doubt.

Temple Resolution:

Replying to the main question by Mr. Chitta Basu (Forward Block), he said that India had made it known that the adoption by Pakistan's national assembly of two resolutions on the temple issue and the situation in Kashmir amounted to interference in India's internal affairs. New Delhi had succeeded in putting across to many important countries that such actions by Pakistan militated against the bid to improve bilateral relations.

Referring to an observation by the BJP leader, Mr. A.B. Vajpayee, that after every meeting between the Prime Ministers of the two countries, some developments took place in Pakistan which worsened bilateral ties, the Prime Minister, Mr. Narasimha Rao, stated that there were forces in every country which were against peace. But such forces were pushed back by those in favour of peace. Also there could be difference of opinion in any country."

The story passes the test of being a news item as any official statement on Indo-Pakistan relations would make news. The lead, however, is not properly brought out. The lead obviously is in the second paragraph where the Minister of State for External Affairs is quoted as saying that India is committed to a dialogue with Pakistan with the aim of improving relations but without compromise on fundamental issues. Out item can be somewhat as follows:

The Minister of state for External Affairs, Mr. Eduardo Faleiro, said -today that India is committed to a dialogue to improve relations with Pakistan. Mr. Faleiro, however, said there will be not compromise on fundamental issues.

He was replying to questions in the Lok Sabha (Lower house of Parliament). The Minister said there was no contradiction between the desire for a dialogue with Pakistan and opposition to Pakistan's support to the terrorists in India. Many countries are now convinced of Pakistan's support to terrorism and some even appear to favour declaring Pakistan a terrorist state.

Intervening, the Prime Minister said that there are forces in every country which are against peace. Mr. Narasimha Rao was referring to a remark by the BJP member, Mr. Atal Bihari Vajpayee, that after every meeting between the Prime Ministers of India and Pakistan a development took place in Pakistan which made the bilateral ties worse. The Prime Minister said there are also forces in favour of peace which push the opposite forces back."

You would notice that the words are around 150. The length is justified because of the importance of the subject. The Prime Minister's intervention makes the story all the more interesting.

Now we tackle two officials handouts, one of which is easy to deal with and the other a little difficult. As we have seen, the official publicity material and statements by major political parties may contain newsy information but need substantial rewriting. There are some important events which newsmen are not permitted to cover and the official releases may become the only sources of information as in the case of the second example taken up below:

The First handout:

"The National Wastelands Development Board was established in May, 1985 with a mandate to undertake development of wastelands through massive programme of afforestation and tree planting with people's participation for achieving the following goals:

Tree planting/afforestation over an area of 10.640 million hectare was achieved against the target of 10.256 million hectare and 265.50 crore seedlings have been distributed against the target of 400.00 crore seedlings upto 1991-92.

There are differing estimates of .wastelands. The National Wastelands Development Board has estimated the area of wastelands at 120 mha whereas the estimate of the Society for Promotion of Wastelands Development is 130 mha.

No targets for land conversion have yet been envisaged by the reconstituted National Wastelands Development Board for the Eighth Five Year Plan.

This information was given by Col. Rao Ram Singh, Minister of State for Wastelands Development, in a written reply to a question by Sh. V. Narayansamy in Rajya Sabha today."

The handout contains a little bit of information. But to convert it into a news item the lead has to be located. The handout leads with a point which is more background than news.

The lead for this small story can be found in the achievement of tree planting in the seven years (1985 to 1992) since the Wastelands Development Board was set up. Our item can be as follows:

"Trees have been planted over more than ten million and six hundred thousand hectares of wasteland since 1985. The planting was a little higher than the target. The development of wastelands began on a big scale seven years ago. This information was given by the Minister of State for Wastelands Development, Colonel Ram Singh, in reply to a question in the Rajya Sabha (upper house of Parliament) today. The Minister said no target has been fixed for converting wasteland into farming land in the Eighth plan now under way."

Now the other handout.

"The first Ambassador of Israel to India, His Excellency Mr. Ephraim Dowek presented his credentials to the President Dr. Shanker Dayal Sharma at Rashtrapati Bhawan today.

Welcoming the Ambassador, Dr. Shanker Dayal Sharma said that with India's Ambassador in Israel having presented his Credentials only a few weeks ago, both sides are now in a position to move forward in imparting the necessary momentum to bilateral relations. ''We in India hold in admiration the immense progress that the people of Israel have made, especially in agriculture, irrigation and the technological fields such as solar energy," Dr. Sharma said.

The President said that India, which has consistently advocated the peaceful resolution of all problems, has welcomed the activation of the West Asia Peace Process for a direct dialogue and discussions between the Israeli and Arab delegations. He said that India is hopeful that this historic opportunity will be utilized to find a just and honourable settlement acceptable to all parties concerned and recognizing the legitimate rights and aspirations of all parties engaged in the peace negotiations. As a manifestation of'.the commitment to promoting all efforts in this direction, India is participating in al 5 groups of the multilateral Peace Process.

The President said that the post cold war era has witnessed a rapidly changing international political and economic environment. It has thrown up several new and complex challenges. Simultaneously we have also been provided with a historic opportunity to reshape inter-state relations. In India's view the new structure must be capable of dealing with challenges that are global in nature and capable of responding to the rapidity of changes. However, such an arrangement should be built on an international consensus through a truly democratic and multilateral process, with the participation of equal and sovereign states. He expressed the confidence that our two countries will be able to work in close consultation with each other in meeting the emerging challenges in the international arena.

Mr. Dowek said that India. and Israel, though different in size, population, background and traditions, have much in common and are in many ways bound by similar characteristics.

H.E. Mr. Dowek said that the extended hands of the two nations have finally met and after almost 45 years of estrangement, full diplomatic relations have been established between our two countries. A new era in our relationship is taking-off under auspicious omens and in a particularly propitious international juncture, he said.

Speaking about the latest development in West Asia, the new Ambassador said that winds of change are blowing in the region. The prospects of peace have never been better he said.

Mr. Dowek expressed his country's gratitude that India has agreed to take an active part in the multilateral negotiations. India's wisdom, its wide international experience, its unwavering commitment to world peace as well as its privileged relationship with all parties concerned will, no doubt, be an important asset to the peace process as a whole."

The item clearly is newsworthy as the first ambassador of Israel being officially accredited to the Indian government is of considerable news value. The handout has also brought out the main point in the lead but it needs some redrafting.

The other points to be covered include the remarks made by the President and the ambassador's reply about Indo-Israeli relations and the peace talks on West Asia. The story could even exceed the average length of 100 words as in the following draft:

"In New Delhi today, the first Israeli ambassador to India, Mr. Ephraim Dowek, presented his credentials to President Shankar Dayal Sharma.

Welcoming the envoy, Dr. Sharma said now that both countries have their ambassadors in each other's capital bilateral relations can be given the needed momentum. In the post-cold war era, he was confident that the two countries can work together. in meeting the challenges in the world. The President said India is hopeful that the West Asia peace talks will result in a just and honourable settlement recognizing the rights and aspirations of all parties.

In his reply, Mr. Dowek said Israel is grateful to India for its active role in the peace talks. In his view prospects for peace in West Asia have never been better as the winds of change are blowing in the region. The ambassador said the hands of India and Israel have met after 45 years of estrangement and a new era is taking off in their relations. Mr. Dowek said India and Israel are different in many ways but have much in common."

For the bulletins going on the air soon after the presentation of credentials this length may be justified. Later in the day the story may be pruned down to 100 words or less. For bulletins directed to foreign listeners, West Asia in particular, the complete story should, however, be taken. Such are the requirements of different bulletins.

Normally the presentation of credentials by a new ambassador, replacing another in a routine transfer, is hardly news. But in the context of India's decision to regularize her ties with Israel after so many years this event was of considerable significance.

In all the stories drafted by us above the essentials of radio/TV newswriting have been carefully borne in mind the brevity of the story, while covering all significant points, giving the item a proper lead, use of simple words and short sentences to conform to the needs of the spoken word medium and introducing variation wherever possible.

You must have also noticed that we have not used the past tense while converting the direct into indirect form. For example, we have said: "The President said India is hopeful." not was hopeful. Or "Mr. Dowek, in his reply, said Israel is grateful." not was grateful.

Some liberty is taken here with grammar because we are using the spoken word medium. The listener may otherwise get the impression that we are referring to some past event if we said "India was hopeful" or *Israel* was grateful."

Also we have avoided repetition wherever possible. The President referred to West Asia peace talks, so in the Israeli ambassador's reply, which follows immediately, we only mentioned "peace talks," not West Asia peace talks. But in the next sentence we had to make it clear that the reference was to West Asia peace talks by mentioning 'prospects for peace in west Asia.' Otherwise, there was a danger of peace being interpreted as world peace.

Repetition has to be avoided, but not at the cost of clarity. Intensive practice is required so that these and other essential points of radio newswriting are grasped and mastered.

EXERCISES:

1. Take up a few stories from the daily papers and rewrite them as Radio/TV news items.
2. Listen carefully to the Radio/TV news bulletins and make a list of stories in writing which the guidelines have not been followed.
3. Report a meeting or any other news event as though you were doing it for Radio/TV.

Chapter V

THE STRUCTURE OF BULLETINS

A number of news item put together makes a news bulletin. But a bulletin is not just a string of individual news items broadcast at the scheduled time. The bulletin is more than a sum total of a number of stories. The bulletin is a collective form in which the separate news items are brought into a coherent order and some relationship.

Every news broadcast is part of the day's broadcasting schedule and there are usually several bulletins in a day's broadcasting output. A newspaper appears only once a day. Although it may have several editions, early city, late city, first dak, second dak and so on, the reader gets only one edition. The radio is often on the air bringing you the latest news every time.

Even in certain programmes of limited duration there is generally a news bulletin. Such programmes are beamed to foreign audiences, in the national network's external or overseas services, with a duration of an hour or sometimes shorter than that. There are also programmes meant for what are called in radio parlance "minority audiences" at home, like the youth and women, or farmers and the armed forces, tribal communities and so on.

No radio programme can be conceived without its component of a news bulletin of general or special interest. Likewise, there cannot be a bulletin for its own sake. You cannot broadcast a bulletin and then go off the air until the next bulletin, except in grave national emergencies. Even then some kind of music or other programmes would still be broadcast along with the news.

Bulletins are generally put out in a series or cycle like AIR's 0815, 1400, 1800 and 2100 hours English bulletins and their Hindi counterparts at 0800, 1410, 1805 and 2045 hours. In addition, AIR has hourly bulletins round the clock in the two languages.

The Indian radio network also has morning, afternoon and evening bulletins in a number of major Indian languages and morning and evening bulletins in some others. Like their English and Hindi counterparts, these are also "national" bulletins, in the sense that they cover national and world news, unlike the regional bulletins from the various stations which cover mainly their state news. The national bulletins are beamed from Delhi and relayed by the respective stations in the linguistic area concerned. The English and Hindi bulletins are relayed by a much larger number of stations, a couple of them by practically all stations in the network.

Each bulletin has its target audience. The editor has to bear in mind the requirements, interests and preferences of the various regions and audiences while preparing his bulletin.

The regional or local bulletins from the stations cover the news from within that state and sometimes from an area within a state. They are really the local bulletins of AIR. For the tribal communities in north-east India, and Himachal Pradesh and Jammu and Kashmir, in the north-west there are special bulletins in the tribal dialects. They are a blend of national and regional news.

This information should help you to understand that a bulletin forms part of a programme.

We may also take note here of AIR's POOL system operating in the General Newsroom (GNR) in Delhi for the past four decades and more. At the Pool desk all copy -

agency messages, reporters' stories, monitoring reports and handouts - is pooled and tasted by a senior editor. He is called the editor-in-charge of the GNR. The selected stories, considered usable by him, are then passed on to two editors assisting him. Together with the editor-in-charge, they rewrite the material as radio news items which are then issued in two Pools, Indian or Home and Foreign. There is also a Sports Pool in the evening hours when there is a heavy fall of sports stories from within and also from without the country. When the two houses of Parliament are in session there is also a Parliament Pool.

The GNR is never closed and the pool works in four shifts round the clock - Morning (0300-0930), Day (0900-1530), Evening (1500-2130) and Night (2100-0330).

The edited and rewritten Pool items are circulated to the bulletin editors called compilation editors because they compile bulletins for broadcast, either direct in English or Hindi, or for translation from English into the respective language of broadcast by another set of trained newsmen who broadcast the bulletin in their language.

The compilation editor has at his disposal the complete pools from the previous shifts. (After each shift the Pool stories are put together with a table of contents).There are besides the incoming stories of the current Pool. Each item in the Pool is circulated as soon as it is finished. Thus an editor doing a bulletin in the evening hours will have before him: The Day Pool I and the Day Pool II of that day, the bulletins done by his colleagues in the series in the morning and the day, *plus* the current stories coming out of the Pool. He can also consult the morning Pools.

All this study enables him to decide what he has to cover in his bulletin from the material already issued by the pool. He has, of course, to cope with the current Pool's flow which can be fast and heavy in the evening hours when most of the Home stories are in.

The Pool system has many advantages from the point of view of a compiling editor, apart from helping the bosses to keep an eye on the flow of stories which would ultimately go into various bulletins. It lightens the burden of the compilation editor and relieves him of the onerous task of wading through acres of agency copy, the heavy bulk of reporters' copy (AIR has a little more than 100 staffers and some 250 stringers) and a wealth of monitoring reports.

It, however, kills part of his initiative. His editorial skill is not put to full use because he does not need to go to the sources. There is nothing though to prevent him from looking at the source material. He has, of course, to subject the Pool copy to further editing, polish the drafts and make the items as acceptable to his audience as possible, besides compiling an interesting bulletin.

So, he has to grasp the essentials of the structure of a bulletin. A radio bulletin is generally divided into four parts:

1. *Headlines,* also referred to as the main points;
2. The *body of the bulletin* which consists of different news items;
3. The *break* which occurs midway, roughly after the first half or bunch of the bulletin, or the first five minutes of a ten minute bulletin. This enables the newsreader to identify the broadcasting station which is a requirement since several stations are on the air on frequencies close to one another. "This is All India Radio giving you the news" is the usual form. This also makes it possible for the news reader to take a deep breath; and
4. The *headlines being repeated* at the end of the bulletin after which comes the closing announcement "that is

the end of the news" or "that is the end of this bulletin".

The announcer of the station then chimes in and tells you:

"You have been listening to a bulletin relayed from Delhi. This is the Jaipur or Trivandrum station of AIR."

A standard radio bulletin is of ten minutes duration. There are bulletins of five minutes also. They generally do not have headlines The hourly bulletins broadcast by AIR are of five minutes duration.

For years AIR had two fifteen minute bulletins, in English and Hindi, in the morning and evening hours. The duration of the morning bulletins was cut to ten minutes several years ago (now reduced to even less than ten minutes) but the evening fifteen minute bulletins have continued to be broadcast. In the context of the stiff competition from TV, specially in the evening hours, how this newscast should shape in future is beyond the scope of this discussion.

The repeating of headlines at the end of a ten minute bulletin and also the fifteen minute one (which has two breaks) is intended to help the listener who may tune in while your broadcast is already on the air and may thus miss the headlines at the start. It also helps you to recapitulate and sum up important stories and indicate to the listener that you are now nearing the end.

The TV follows the same pattern with the difference that it is possible for it to add visuals or captions even while the headlines are being repeated. But it has no break.

The radio system of a break almost midway is a good device to divide the stories into two recognizable sections. But there can never be any hard and fast rule that home or foreign stories would form part of the first or second bunch.

The arrangement of items in a bulletin requires considerable skills and editorial ability. This is where the point made at the beginning of this chapter that a bulletin is more than the total of its items becomes relevant. The stories have to be integrated to the extent this is possible.

For example, all stories about a major national development or an important international event have to be taken together, as far as possible. They have to be brought into a compact form, repetition being avoided. This is to be done in such a way that after the main news in the story the repercussions, comments and reactions, along with any offshoot or sequel, are arranged in a logical and interesting manner.

Let us suppose there is a story about the Supreme Court of India directing the State Government of Uttar Pradesh (UP) that no construction be allowed to be done at Ayodhya, the town where the disputed shrine exists, for building a new Rama temple, until the stay issued by the state high court remains in force. The Supreme Court ordered on November 22, 1992 that 'Kar Seva' (religious voluntary work) in Ayodhya be only symbolic in nature.

Now this would naturally be your lead, certainly of the long Ayodhya story on that day and possibly of your entire bulletin. After the main court verdict, you have to take any discussion on the subject in Parliament, comments by political parties and the State Government and the Central Government and other related stories. The arrival of any volunteers in Ayodhya could also be reported alongside and a voiced despatch by your correspondent summing up the situation and the fallout could also follow.

In the newspapers, all these stories would be different items, with their headings, and placed alongside the main story or even separately on different pages. Not so in the radio (or TV). In our media you have to bring all the related stories together in the form of a roundup, avoiding unnecessary repetitions and reducing the less important stories to the barest minimum so that the overall story is not too long. Yet it should be as comprehensive as possible.

This arrangement is called for when there is a major story to be handled. Even otherwise, related items should be brought into some in kind of linkage. However, while integrating stories care should be taken not to play up stories which may have some loose connection with the major item but by themselves they may not be significant.

If for example, there is a major story about the western nations conferring, along with Japan, on how to help Russia out of its economic difficulties and you have a story on a Russian delegation visiting India or Italy for trade talks it is not necessary for you to place it alongside the major item. If there is time you can deal with it later in the bulletin.

The point made here is that *integration is necessary* but an *artificial integration is unjustified.* The story is told of an editor in AIR who first covered a story on the late N. Gopalaswamy Ayyangar, an important minister in the first Jawaharlal Nehru cabinet, and then tried to integrate it with another story. “Meanwhile another Gopalaswamy, the registrar general of India, ... ” Such unnatural linkage is uncalled for and laughter-provoking.

That also helps us to emphasize that stories must be taken in the bulletin in the order of their importance, with sports stories coming at the end. There is no set rule on the bifurcation of home and foreign stories. The comparative importance of home and foreign stories has to be judged in the context of the available newsfall.

If an international story - like a stock exchange crisis in the world financial capitals, the Somalia starvation crisis leading to UN troops intervention, inauguration .of the US President - deserves priority over the home stories, go ahead by all means and lead with it. But that would not justify some other less important foreign stories being played up along with it, just for the sake of taking foreign stories together. The news importance of each story would decide its place, in the final analysis.

As we have seen, the Pool helps the compilation editor in AIR considerably. This does not mean the bulletin editor should not further edit the Pool copy or take it as final and sacrosanct. The contents must not be altered without the editor-in-charge being consulted but the language and presentation must be suitably touched up and even the lead can be altered.

The compilation editor is the one who prepares the final product which goes on the air. (The actual delivery is in the hands, or the voice, of the newsreader.) So the bulletin editor must ensure that he gives each item a proper shape and strings them together like beads in a rosary. The stories must not sound as though they have been jumbled up.

The bulletin editor has to bear in mind the need for variation. If the Pool has led two items with the usual lead "so-and-so has said.. " you can vary the lead of the second item. Thus, you can say, "The government's policy on the basis of settling the industrial dispute in the Indian Airlines between the pilots and the management was explained in the Lok Sabha (lower house of Parliament) today by the Civil Aviation minister." This would reduce the monotony of 'so-and-so has said...'

Where no linkage is possible you have to demarcate one item from another so that the listener knows you are now on to something else. This can be done by beginning your new item with words like "In Bombay today ... " "At the United Nations" or "back home in the Madhya Pradesh Assembly" if you are reverting to home stories after a detour of foreign items.

Confusion should not be allowed to be created in the

listener's mind. Such confusion can arise even in headlines if the identity of the individual quoted by you is not properly brought out.

Sports items, which must form an important part of your bulletin, any bulletin for that matter, should be demarcated from the other stories by introducing the story or stories with word like "Now Sport" or "Cricket" or "Hockey," as the case may be.

Sports, like weather, is taken at the end of the bulletin but care must be taken not to "crowd out" the sports stories, that is end the bulletin without broadcasting the stories. In the technical language of broadcasting, stories which you have included in your bulletin with the intention of broadcasting them but which you had to leave out for want of time are called "crowded out" items. For record and for the guidance of the succeeding editors in the series, the CO stories must be clearly indicated. You should however, note that while you can take some solace that you had intended to cover them the listener has not got the story. It is thus as good as a story not covered.

If a sports story has been headlined you must make sure that it is broadcast. It is inexcusable to leave out a headline story.

Headlines are like the display in the shop window, revealing enough to attract the shopper but holding back a lot. It is a kind of strip-tease. Headlines should be crisp, short and must not carry too many details. At the same time the headline must not be vague, like "India, is waging a grim battle in the second test at Johannesburg." You should rather tell the listener what the grim battle is about. "At Johannesburg India is 100 for four with half a day left before the match ends."

In broadcasting organizations where the Pool system does not obtain and the editor has to draft his bulletin from the source material direct he has to bear in mind all the points made about newswriting as well as compilation. He has to deploy his editorial skills to the best advantage and use such assistance as is available. Naturally he has to start his work pretty early, earlier than his counterparts in AIR, but he can use all the freedom and latitude that is available to him as well as he can.

The stories drafted by such editors become a kind of standard to be followed by succeeding editors and those doing other bulletins until after a few hours when his bulletin becomes outdated. Then someone else does the same spadework.

The hourly bulletins do not have headlines. There is not enough time for headlines as their duration is short. A ten minute bulletin should generally have four headlines and five are enough for a fifteen minute newscast. Only when a major story deserves two headlines you should exceed this limit. Remember more headlines, which have again to be repeated at the end, mean less time for the body of the bulletin.

The bulletin proper must begin with the lead headline story, which is the lead of your bulletin. Sometimes a newscast begins with a story which has not been headlined but is otherwise considered important. That is a wrong practice, not to be emulated. If the story deserves to be taken first in the bulletin why not lead with it in the headlines?

Besides the lead story, there should be at least one headline story in the first bunch of your bulletin. The second bunch can open with the third or fourth headline, unless the fourth headline is about a sports story in which case the story has to come at the end of the bulletin. In a fifteen minute bulletin it should be your effort to open the third bunch with a headline story.

The sports stories come towards the end but if there is a

major victory in international sports for your home team or an athlete has won laurels in the Olympic games the bulletin can be led with it.

Here are a few samples of Pool items of AIR:

Andhra CM:

The Andhra Pradesh Chief Minister, Mr. Janardhana Reddy has decided to step down. The AICC{I) General Secretary in charge of Andhra Pradesh, Mr. Janardhana Poojary, told our correspondent this evening that the Congress (I) President, Mr. P.V. Narasimha Rao, has accorded permission sought by Mr. Reddy to step down from the Chief Ministership. Mr. Poojary said Mr. Narasimha Rao has also instructed Mr. Janardhana Reddy to submit his resignation as soon as the appropriation bill is passed in the state assembly which is now in session. The Congress (I) President has also placed on record his appreciation of the contributions made by Mr. Reddy as Chief Minister of Andhra Pradesh. He also complimented Mr. Reddy for the respect he has shown for the high values and traditions of the Congress, Mr. Poojary said. Panigrahi 1715 hours"

Lead agreement:

India and Britain have signed an Extradition Treaty and an agreement on confiscation of terrorists' property and assets. A spokesman of the Indian High commission in London informed the AIR newsroom on telephone a short while ago that the visiting Home Minister, Mr. S.B.Chavan, and his British counterpart, Mr. Kenneth Clarke, signed the treaty this evening. According to the treaty, Britain will not allow the anti-India extremists to operate from its territory."

Harshad Mehta:

Stock broker Harshad Mehta has been set free after 110 days of detention.

Mr. Mehta, the prime accused in the securities scandal, was freed today by the Bombay High Court directly after Mr. Justice M.L. Dudhat held that he be released since there is no order against him for his arrest or detention in any other case. Earlier Mr. Mehta had filed an application before the High Court stating that he is being illegally detained without any valid order in violation of the court order yesterday.

The High court had yesterday confirmed the bail order of Mr. Mehta passed by the Additional Chief Metropolitan Magistrate on the ninth of this month, rejecting the Enforcement Directorate's plea. The Byculla district jail authorities had, however, refused to release Mr. Mehta stating that he was required in New Delhi in connection with 'the corruption case against former Planning Commission member, Mr. V. Krishnamoorthy. In his order the judge said further detention of Mr. Mehta will be patently illegal.

EXERCISES:

1. In the Pool items given above find out errors of omission and commission.
2. Listen carefully to radio and TV bulletins and critically examine the contents from the point of view of the structure of a bulletin.
3. What are the essentials of a good bulletin?

Chapter VI

COMPILING A BULLETIN

Having grasped the structure of a news bulletin we now move on to the compilation of bulletins and see what all it involves.

Either you have a Pool to present you with broadcastable stories on a platter, as in AIR, or you to have compile the bulletin from the sources of news direct. In either case there is plenty of material at your disposal. This requires that you begin your work of writing or drafting stories fairly early so that you know at the start what is already there and what you can anticipate.

For a ten minute bulletin the editor must begin this work at least 2½ hours before the time of broadcast. If you are doing one of the fifteen minute bulletins the work must begin 3½ hours prior to the broadcast.

This time must be further advanced by an hour if you are doing the bulletin direct from the sources. For a five minitue bulletin done from the Pool items the time must be an hour before the scheduled time of going on the air and another half an hour if the editor is relying on the sources.

But before he sets out to write the stories for broadcast the editor must spend an hour (add half an hour for a fifteen minitue bulletin) studying the material that is already available. The previous Pools, Day Pool I and II and both the Morning Pools, along with the previous bulletins of the cycle, would constitute the material. In the other case, 'the editor has to study not only the previous bulletins of the series but also the agency copy, reporters' copy and monitoring reports received since the last bulletin went on the air.

The related copy material must be pinned together, under different 'broad headings, like "Ayodhya", "Parliament", "European Community" or "Sports". Some AIR editors are also habituated to pin together related Pool items so that they can easily locate the stories while rewriting the items.

The material thus studied naturally constitutes the sheet anchor of the stories to be put together into the bulletin. But the editor has also to cope with the incoming copy as he gets down to drafting his stories. This is the most difficult part of his job as the flow of Pool copy or source material may go on increasing in intensity while you are concentrating on the task of drafting. Particularly the pressure of home stories mounts in the evening hours as almost all the main home stories land during these hours or some time before.

The agency tickers are ticking away, the reporters' copy keeps piling up and the foreign stations are being monitored as the bulletin editor is busy at his desk. Not only has he to look at all the incoming stories quickly and decide what he is going to do with them he has also to bring these new stories in relation to the ones he may have selected from the material studied by him. Often a big story lands while you are actually engaged in writing your bulletin and this may materially alter the scheme of things you have decided for yourself. The lead may also have to be changed sometimes.

The bulletin is, therefore, compiled piecemeal, not in the order in which it is broadcast. The similarity with the shooting of a feature film or documentary is thus striking. A film is never shot in the order in which it is viewed by the audience in a cinema or at home on the video. The shots and rushes are brought into (hopefully) a coherent order by the film editor under his director's instructions.

But the film director has at least a script to go by and while the hero or heroine, as often happens in Hindi movies, may force him to alter some parts to grab the juicy breaks he at least knows what is being shot according to his script. The bulletin editor, on the other hand, does not have a script at his disposal.

To some extent this lacuna is made good by the daily editorial meeting which obtains in AIR and several broadcasting organisations. In this meeting, attended by the main evening bulletin editors with the senior bosses of the network, a stock is taken of all the available stories and what is anticipated on the basis of information about the likely developments. The lead and possible headlines and some other major points are broadly decided in that get-together.

For other periods of the day or early morning, less formal consultations take place over the phone or in face-to-face discussion.

By no stretch of imagination this can, however, be called scripting because some stories may break without notice which may render any predetermined scheme wholly untenable. The meetings and consultations help in identifying the major items before the editor sits down to write his bulletin. The inter-relation of the items and their comparative importance is also clarified and the editor gets to know what he can anticipate by way of fresh news fall.

The editor has, however, to have sufficient resilience of mind and be ready to accommodate a totally unexpected story in his bulletin - a natural disaster of immense proportions, at home or in the neighbourhood of your country, a terrorist strike of unusual magnitude, the death of a highly important person which may have political repercussions and so on. This may alter your basic pattern and change the lead you may have decided upon at the meeting. That is all part of the game.

However, the editor has to avoid infructuous work as far as he can. This saves him considerable effort and energy and also puts less strain on his colleagues, including the stenographer who is typing out the bulletin at top speed and his editorial colleague who may be helping him with some drafting. What is more important, if your bulletin is being translated into a different language, one of the home languages or a foreign language, you must bear in mind the strain caused to the translators by extra effort that would be needed for translating fresh material while well edited and translated matter is thrown away.

Like the English and Hindi bulletins in AIR, some bulletins are broadcast in the language in which they have been written. Some others, in fact, many more, are translated from a basic English script. The translators grumble if they have to discard translated material from day to day. They would bear with you and cooperate if you impose such burden on them only now and then. The translators also have to realise that they are part of the news organisation and they must stand ready to accommodate fresh and interesting stories related to unexpected developments.

Interaction between the compiling editor and the news units in different languages would, on the one hand, help them to know what is coming their way and what is expected and, on the other, the translating units will also get into the spirit of the bulletin making process, rather than remain passive translators.

The need to impose the least possible strain on the translators and on one's colleagues will be well taken care of .f the bulletin editor follows a certain drill. He must first take up for drafting stories which are more or less final.

He may begin with the weather story, which is a must and which is the routine daily weather report and forecast. Sometimes the weather itself becomes a major item when it turns particularly bad, there is a heat wave or cold wave on or there is a cyclonic storm. Such stories have to be given prominence and even headlined. The routine weather story comes towards the end of the bulletin and is generally carried with the introduction "and now the weather".

Finally the editor has to handle the major stories and take into account the additional news fall during his tenure. This must be properly integrated with the material that has undergone editing and was pending since he arrived in the newsroom. Among such stories would, of course, be the lead of the bulletin. In AIR the Pool comes to the help of the bulletin editors by issuing to them a roundup of some major story or stories. The bulletin editors have to keep in touch with the Pool to know what is coming. This practice is necessary even otherwise.

The lead of your bulletin and the headlines should be decided while you are drafting the early stories and after the incoming stories are scrutinised. While the lead story is left over to be handled towards the end, possible headlines can and should be drafted on a separate notesheet. Two or three more than the number prescribed should be jotted down and polished as you are getting different stories ready.

Such preparations help you to approach the important task of dictating the headlines in an unhurried manner. Coolness and methodical work is called for in ample measure. The notepad can also be used for noting down the stories you may consider as possible usable items and also for noting down the items which would go into the two or three bunches into which your bulletin is divided. As important news breaks the notes can also be altered but if you do not have anything to fall back upon and depend only on your mental notes you would cause unnecessary problems for yourself in the final hour which is crucial.

The last half hour should be reserved for

(1) Dictating the headlines, (2) Arrangement of the items in the order in which they are to be broadcast and dividing them into two bunches (three for a fifteen minute bulletin); and (3) Accommodating a possible last minute story which has to be covered without headlining.

For the translating units, the "order of items" has to be made available to them along with the headlines half an hour before the broadcast. The order must indicate the division of items into bunches.

As for the English bulletin, the editor has to arrange the pages and number them serially according to the order he has decided upon. In the process called "bunching" some typed pages may have to be torn into bits if two or more items have been typed on them. Thus, sometimes a "page" of the bulletin being read is nothing more but four or five lines.

As the broadcast time approaches some editors display nerves. There is a rigid discipline of starting broadcasts on time and news bulletins are often preceeded by the time signal by which people set their watches. You have, therefore, to be ready with the news pages before the pips are sounded. The newsreader has to rehearse all the pages, including the headlines page, and go to the studio from where the newscast is to be put out. He has also to approach his task with utmost calm and coolness although he is usually under some tension.

The editor can enjoy the thrill and sensation of the process of bulletin making if he keeps a cool head all the time. There is no reason why the enjoyment should be denied to anyone if the drill we have recommended here is followed. The editor has to go to the studio and help the newsreader by making adjustments in the order of items, asking him to drop the less essential ones if he is running out of time, or give him some additional material if he is falling short.

The newsreader should be allowed to rehearse the entire bulletin but he must also be prepared to read something, now and then, without rehearsing. He must not act fussy but the editor must also bear his mental state in mind and cause the least disturbance in his work. Any changes made by the editor after the pages have been rehearsed must be brought to the notice of the reader as far as possible.

It is customary for the TV news presentors to smile at you as he or she calls the end of the newscast. This may be just good manners or part of TV's effort to please the audience but in the case of the news staff this is a genuine expression of relief that it is all over without any hitch. The radio newsreader is all keyed up while he is getting ready to broadcast and during the bulletin but his relief at the end of the broadcast has to be seen to be believed.

A bulletin is never finished until the end is announced. The radio being an instant medium can bring to you news as it happens and several bits can be added as the broadcast is on the air. So, everyone has to be ready—the editor, his supporting staff, the newsreader—to incorporate into the bulletin any important story or aspects of a story which materially alter or add to the one you have done.

Interaction between the compiling editor and the newsreader on the one hand and. the editor and the translating unit on the other cannot be over emphasised, The newsreader is the person who delivers. the final product and since it is he who reads your bulletin he is better placed to judge the spoken word aspects of the stories. His suggestions should, therefore, be well received and accepted to the extent possible. A simpler or softer word here and a more conversational phrase there can enliven your bulletin.

At the same time, the reader must not take it upon himself to alter anything in the bulletin except correcting typographical errors. He must consult the editor before making changes of a drafting nature or factual kind.

The news readers are expected to read the bulletin at a uniform speed, neither too fast nor too slow, so that the editor knows how many words (or typed lines) would be needed. But he has to make allowance for the fact that there can be small variations in speed between a news reader and another. He has thus to keep more news material ready for a reader reputed to be a speeding and somewhat less for one who is known to drag his feet or Voice.

All points made in the previous chapter about the structure of a bulletin have to be borne in mind. These include the rule that headline items must not be left out and to avoid this such items must not be placed towards the very end. Sports stories must be indicated as "must" and the news reader told not to miss them.

The items which are crowded out must be marked "C.O." and two diagonal parallel lines drawn across them. This would convey to the succeeding editor that these items were considered worthy of broadcasting by you but they could not be covered for want of time. For record also it is essential that the "C.O." markings be there in the record copy of the bulletin.

The succeeding editor may still find them useful if they have not been outdated. In the radio the stories get outdated after a few hours. You must, however, remember that it is no comfort to the listeners that something was considered fit for coverage but was left out as "C.O." The listener has missed the story or stories and that is all that matters. In other words, all that you consider "fit to broadcast" must be covered.

Given below for your information, is a complete morning English bulletin of AIR. In 1991, AIR changed the format of the morning news, making it a fifteen minute programme consisting of a news bulletin, a short news commentary and a brief roundup of the daily press. This means the bulletin duration has been slightly reduced from the normal ten minutes devoted to the morning bulletin. But otherwise the pattern of a ten minute newscast, headlines, two bunches, almost equally divided, a break and repeating of headlines, has not changed. The headlines are repeated as the "main points of the bulletin" at the end of the fifteen minute "Morning News" programme, after the commentary and the roundup of the morning papers.

Now the bulletin:

ALL INDIA RADIO M.R.S. Menon: D.S. Saini: Arvind

News Services Division 30.11.1992

English - 0815 hours

GOOD MORNING

First we bring you the news followed by a commentary on "Need for speedy Transition in South Africa". And now over to Baron Haldar for the news.

Security arrangements are being further tightened in and around the disputed site at Ayodhya in view of the proposed "kar seva". The District and Sessions Judge of Moradabad has been appointed observer to monitor the situation.

In Andhra Pradesh, a superintendent of police has been killed by suspected militants near Hyderabad.

A Chinese Parliamentary delegation is arriving in the capital today on a nine day visit to India.

The fourth Asian junior track and field meet opens in New Delhi today.

Security arrangements are being further tightened in and around the disputed complex at Ayodhya in view of the proposed kar seva. According to police sources, the Faizabad district administration has asked for more companies of PAC.

Meanwhile the RSS has said that the kar sevaks will honour the Supreme Court judgment and will perform only pooja and yagya at Ayodhya. The RSS joint secretary, Mr Rajendra Singh, told newsmen in Chandigarh that the sevaks have been directed not to start any construction work.

The BJP has alleged that the centre is planning to take action against the Uttar Pradesh government and said it can lead to serious consequences. The party Vice-President, Mr Sikandar Bakht, and General Secretary, Mr Madan Lal Khurana, said in New Delhi that the centre is deliberately delaying a decision on the Ayodhya issue.

The District and Sessions Judge of Moradabad, Mr Tej Shankar, will proceed to Moradabad today.

The national plan of action for the SAARC decade of the girl child and a legal literacy manual for women are being released at a meeting in New Delhi today. The meeting has been convened to discuss the rising trend of atrocities against women. The meeting will be attended by women members of Parliament, members of the national commission for women and senior officials. The action plan prepared by the government focuses on the three major goals of survival, protection and development of the girl child in India while emphasising the needs of girl children belonging to special and vulnerable groups and adolescent girls.

The Andhra Pradesh Chief Minister, Mr Vijaya Bhaskara Reddy, has said that the state is interested in setting up new coal-based power plants with foreign participation. He was talking to a four member Ukrainian delegation in Hyderabad. The leader of the delegation, Mr Dennis A. Zgursky, told the Chief Minister that Ukraine is ready to collaborate with India in the setting up of electronics, machine building and power plants.

A Chinese Parliamentary delegation is arriving in New Delhi today on a nine day visit to India. The delegation is led by the Vice Chairman of the National People's Congress standing committee, Mr Liao Han Sheng.

During its stay, the delegation will call on the Vice President, the Prime Minister and the Lok Sabha Speaker. It will also visit Agra, Madras, and Bombay. The delegation will also participate in the Festival of China to be held in the capital.

France has confirmed that the agreement for the supply of a French nuclear power plant to Pakistan will be signed shortly. This was announced by the French ambassador to Pakistan, Mr Jean Pierre Messet, while talking to news persons in Lahore yesterday. He said the Pakistan government should take steps to sign the non-proliferation treaty soon.

This is All India Radio giving you the news.

In Andhra Pradesh, a superintendent of police and a constable were shot dead by suspected militants on the outskirts of Hyderabad yesterday. According to the police, Mr Krishna Prasad, SP of special investigation bureau, along with three constables rushed to a house following a tip off. When they entered the house the militants opened fire killing the SP and one constable on the spot. The State Home Minister and senior officials rushed to the spot and investigations are on.

The Haryana Chief Minister, Mr Bhajan Lal, has urged the freedom fighters to help the government in fostering nationalism, by rejuvenating their patriotic spirit. Mr Bhajan Lal was speaking in Hissar after unveiling a statue of Shaheed Udham Singh. The Chief. Minister said that the youth should be enthused to devote their energies towards national reconstruction programmes.

In Punjab, the self-styled Lt. General of a militant organisation, Kulvinder Singh, along with his two accomplices was killed in an encounter with the security forces last night near village ASSIKALAN in Ludhiana district. Two rifles, one revolver and two kilograms of explosive materials were recovered from them. In another encounter near a village in Jalandhar district one militant Nishad Ahmed Sheikh of Srinagar was arrested by the security forces.

The African National Congress has confirmed that members of its military wing are still being sent to other countries for military training. Speaking on South African Television, the ANC general secretary, Mr Ramapoza said that the aim was not to train them for guerrilla warfare but to train them for eventual integration into a new South African army.

Meanwhile African national Congress President, Dr Nelson Mandela, has reiterated that his party will not agree with the government's proposal to hold elections in April 1994. Addressing a large gathering in Namatadi near Pretoria, Dr. Mandela said that they waited for over three hundred years for liberation and they cannot do it any longer.

Latest reports from Venezuela say that at least one hundred and seventy people were killed in Friday's coup attempt. According to Defense Minister, Mr. Ivan Jimenez, over one hundred forty two civilians and twenty seven armed personnel were massacred. Mr. Jimenez added that one thousand two hundred rebel troops including five hundred officers have been arrested following the second military uprising in the country in ten months.

In Peru, at least twenty rebels were killed in an attack on a military base in the north-east of the capital Lima. Three soldiers were also killed in the encounter.

The Russian President Mr. Yeltsin, has urged his followers to set up a new political party with a view to rallying support for radical reforms in the country. Talking to newsmen in Moscow he said that the continuing programmes of radical reforms needed a strong base in society and an appropriate structure.

The former Soviet leader, Mr. Mikhail Gorbachev, has criticised the Russian President Mr. Boris Yeltsin, for trying to go too fast on economic reforms and forcing a change on the people. Mr. Gorbachev, now on a private visit to Argentina, told reporters in Buenos Aires Mr. Yeltsin its seeking to totally privatise the economy in a year when it took. Stalin four years to collectivise agriculture.

Noted choreographer of the Raigarh gharana, Pundit Firtu Maharaj, died at Rajghat in Madhya Pradesh yesterday. He was 71.

The fourth Asian junior track and field meet commences in New Delhi today. Over four hundred athletes representing twenty-four countries are taking part in the meet. Hosts India is fielding a 91 member squad to compete in several events.

In Orissa another piece of stone and chunks of plaster fell from the top of the sanctum sanctorum of Jagannath temple at Puri yesterday. The incident occurred when the idols were being shifted to a nearby chamber to facilitate the repair of the temple.

(Then follows a short commentary on a topical issue. Finally a summary of the main news and special features in the Delhi newspapers. Then the headlines again.)

"Before we close here is the news summary;

Security arrangements are being further tightened in and around the disputed site at Ayodhya in view of the proposed kar seva. The District and Sessions Judge of Moradabad has been appointed observer to monitor the situation. The RSS says the kar sevaks will honour the Supreme Court's judgment and will perform only pooja and Yagya.

A superintendent of Police and a constable were killed by suspected militants on ;the outskirts of Hyderabad yesterday.

A Chinese parliamentary delegation is arriving in the capital today on a nine day visit to India.

The national plan of action for the SAARC decade of the girl child is being released today.

The fourth Asian junior track and field meet opens in Delhi today.

And that is the end of the Morning News.

EXERCISES:

1. What is the drill to be followed by a compilation editor?
2. How does a compilation editor cope with fresh copy while he is writing his bulletin?
3. Critically examine the AIR bulletin reproduced above.

Chapter VII

DIFFERENT TYPES OF BULLETINS

In the previous two chapters we saw how a bulletin is structured and the drill you have to follow in compiling a bulletin. We took the ten minute bulletin as a standard radio news bulletin and examined its features and the features of a fifteen minute bulletin. We also discussed a five minute bulletin briefly.

The ten minute bulletin is, in many ways, a complete news broadcast because it can convey a lot to the listeners. Most radio bulletins, apart from the hourly spot news bulletins, are of ten minutes duration. This goes for several AIR bulletins, in English and Hindi, as well as major Indian languages and several foreign and tribal languages. The world service bulletins of the BBC (British Broadcasting Corporation, broadcasting from London) are of that duration.

The reason is not far to seek. From the point of view of broadcasting and the spoken word limitations, which we have discussed, ten minutes is a resonable time-frame in which you can convey a substantial amount of information, cover all the major stories as well as some less important stories and yet not make the listener feel any strain. Five minutes may be found inadequate and unsatisfying from the polit of view of a good roundup of the news and a fifteen minute bulletin or a longer one would certainly strain the listener's ears and mind.

A ten minute bulletin is designed thus to bring to the listener all the relevant news whether it is scheduled in the morning or evening hours. Of course, the evening bulletin is more newsy, irrespective of the country of broadcast. It is also satisfying from the point of view of the editor and the audience. The reason is that much of the home news is in by the time the bulletin in the evening goes on the air. It goes without saying that any audience would be more interested in home news than news from abroad.

The morning bulletin, on the other hand, often has foreign stories than its evening counterpart and sometimes covers more foreign news than home news. Overnight the agency tickers transmit more stories from abroad than from within the country. The reporters at home also do not have much new material to offer and, of course, the monitoring serviced only bring you news from other countries.

The morning editor has another problem. He knows that the listeners in the metropolitan cities and other big cities and towns which have local newspapers have access to their daily papers. If the evening bulletins have done justice to home news you can say that you have stolen the thunder of the morning papers. But the daily papers generally "go to bed", or get printed, around 2 a.m. or slightly before that, so that they have the opportunity to carry all important foreign stories and sports from abroad in which the home listener is interested.

So, the morning bulletin must give, or appear to give, to the listener something more than what the evening bulletin of that cycle has covered and something more than the morning papers the listener has access to have done. At the same time, an important principle of broadcasting is also to be borne in mind. This is that there would be many listeners who do not have access to the daily papers early in the morning—those in small towns and villages, those in remote military stations and the like—and there may be others who have missed your evening bulletin also. Their interests have thus to be kept in mind.

The principle is that you are not catering only to those who already have some information but to others too who are not so privileged. So your guiding principle is: give whatever is the news at that hour. But you cannot forget that the morning papers are out. So, such stories as were received by about 2 a.m.—must be covered in a manner which would indicate that you are updating them bringing out some new aspects of it. Of course, you have several stories which landed after 2 a.m.—deliberations of the UN Security Council, some developments in the international sphere, late home stories-which you can highlight.

Sometimes you may get a real windfall. On January 17, 1991 when the United States-led armies of the western nations and some of their Muslim allies launched a big military offensive against Iraq almost all the Indian dailies had "gone to bed". They usually do so, the latest by 2 a.m. and the invasion was secretly timed by the American commander for 3-20 a.m.

So, the dailies went without the news of the West Asia or Gulf war having begun. In fact, one prominent daily had come out with a banner headline" "Arabian Desert Quiet but Tense". By the time the paper was in the hands of even the privileged metropolitan readers the desert was burning hot with bombs and missiles. Both AIR and Doordarshan were to put them wise about the war having actually begun.

Such stories do not always come the way of the radio/ TV editors and they have to make do with other stories from home and abroad. One of the advantages, however, they have is in looking forward to the day's major (anticipated) developments. The newspapers, preoccupied as they are with the previous day's news, often do not have much space to devote to the forthcoming events. The radio and TV morning bulletins, however, can bring to their audiences a glimpse of what the day holds for them.

This is an important feature of the morning bulletin-looking at the anticipated developments. The two houses of Parliament may be beginning a crucial session, a non-confidence debate may begin in a state assembly on that day against the state government, or a major sports event may be beginning.

Here a word of caution: some editors tend to overplay the forthcoming events and start talking about them a day or two in advance. By the time they actually come off the listener has been bored stiff and sufficiently annoyed. It is important that this should. not become a routine practice.

The fifteen minute bulletin is, by its duration, more comprehensive in its ,coverage. For years AIR had two such bulletins, in English and Hindi, one each in the morning and evening. However, the morning bulletin was reduced to ten minutes some years ago, partly because there was not much fresh news to give the listener each morning. The problem existed even for a ten minute bulletin but the bigger one was, to so say, cut by one-third at one stroke.

If we recall the events of those early days, after independence, we would find that there was no TV network—Doordarshan's national programme began only in 1983-and there were not many daily papers in existence and neither did they reach out to the readers in the small towns and villages and remote areas. There was thus some justification for a fifteen minute duration.

The evening fifteen minute bulletin had always had, specially in those days, a large following. Many people who believed in the virtue of 'early to bed and early to rise' made it a point of getting the latest on the world and their country before retiring by listening to the 9 p.m. bulletin, Among them was no less a person that the "Iron Man" of India, Sardar Patel, the architect of Indian unity and India's first Deputy Prime Minister who was also for some time Minister of Information and Broadcasting.

The importance of the bulletin was enhanced by the fact that it was the last radio bulletin of the day from the national network, The hourly bulletins came much later.

But fifteen minutes is, in any case, the outer limit of a listener's endurance after which the danger of the listener switching off or going over to some other station arises.

There is no disputing the fact that the fifteen minute bulletin, if well edited and made newsy, can be really comprehensive and interesting. For a federal country like India which is also large and variegated, there is so much to report and such a bulletin would, therefore, appear to fulfil a need. This is specially true of the evening bulletin because, as we have seen, there is much to cover in the evening hours,

But now that there are many rival attractions or distractions with the powerful TV medium and so many competing channels of unalloyed entertainment, the question arises whether there is place for such, a newscast. The 9 p.m. slot is TV's prime time and the question whether the bulletin should continue to be broadcast at that time may soon face the AIR people.

The hourly bulletin which are of five minutes' duration have to satisfy the listener's hunger for the latest information. The news of the moment, also called spot news, must be brought to him along with a coverback of important earlier stories which are still valid and not outdated or timebarred.

We shall examine the five minute bulletins at some length in the following chapter.

The point has already been made earlier that every news bulletin must bear in mind the needs of the fresh listener, the one who may not have heard your bulletins earlier in the series. There are those listeners who could have heard one or more of your previous bulletins and there are others who bring a fresh (not blank) mind to bear on your newscast.

We have to think of both the categories and we cannot do better than follows the dictum: *Every bulletin must project the news of the moment,* no matter whether somebody has heard it before.

Repetition of some of the earlier stories will thus become inevitable. But you have to strive to present the repeated story or stories with a new look. You can make it different by modifying the lead, adding a new point in the lead and a little redrafting of the story without taking anything of substance out of it, or altering the facts and changing the lead.

In any case, you have to coverback on the orginal story while adding a news angle or aspect to it. You must refrain from committing the error which many practising editors fall into of ignoring the major stories on the misunderstanding that what has been reported earlier need not be repeated. They behave as though the event never took place (at least for the bulletings they are compiling.)

Remember that the same listener is not listening to your network's bullethins all the time. The latter's interests are, in any case, taken care of by skilful editing of the earlier stories as we have indicated.

An example will make the point clear. Suppose that the story of the abortive coup against the then Soviet

President, Mikhael Gorbachev, (before he was actually overthrown with the dissolution of the Soviet Union) is received by your newsroom around 1030 hours (as it actually did). In the 1100 hourly bulletin and even the 1200 one the lead has to be "Mr Gorbachev has been overthrown", followed by whatever details are available.

In the 1300 hours bulletin you can attempt a new lead with a possible new point, like the statement by the coup leders about the personal safety of Gorbachev. You can then coverback: "Mr Gorbachev was overthrown in a coup, as already reported." You can add some details about the ouster story.

As the story develops you can vary the lead but by now you can be sure that a very large number of people have already heard the news of his ouster and they would be looking for more details and possibly the Indian government's reaction (which actually carne very late.) If no comments are forthcoming from Delhi or whichever is your country it is essential that you say as much instead of keeping quiet about it.

The instance is, of course, an exceptional one as the ouster story is an extraordinary news item which you do not run into every day. But the drill can be followed with all developing stories, or even others where the lead can be changed internally, in order to satisfy both the habitual listeners and the causal ones.

We have already pointed out the need to bear the audience of your bulletin in mind while compiling it. Each bulletin has its separate audience. The major AIR bulletins in English and Hindi are addressed to a wider "national" audience because of the language used and the fact that the bulletin is made available to listeners in many parts of the country. The bulletins in these two languages are relayed by a large number of stations.

By comparison, the bulletins in the major Indian languages, (miscalled regional languages) are addressed to the people who understand them. The audience is thus considerably restricted and limited.

Some of these bulletins, for audiences speaking the various Indian languages, are clubbed together and a common English script is compiled in the GNR. As many as four languages are thus combined. But the compiling editor has to remember that the listener of each bulletin expects you to give him a complete bulletin with the proper lead and headlines.

For example, the proceedings of the Tamil Nadu assembly may be (in most cases, must be) headlined. It could sometimes be even the lead of that bulletin, depending upon the other newsfall. But it need not necessarily be headlined in the other three bulletins - Kannada, Malayalam, and Telugu. Certainly it cannot be the lead for them, unless the proceedings have been unusual, unruly, uproarious and may have some repercussions on inter-state relations among two or more of the southern states. Such is the audience interest impact on news coverage.

Just as a Tamil Nadu newspaper would highlight the assembly proceedings, even if they have been more or less staid and sober, and they may not find even a mention in the newspapers in the three other languages, the radio bulletins in the four languages must reflect the needs and interests of the audience not in a separatist but a realistic and audience-oriented media approach.

There are a variety of other bulletins - youth, sports, special weather bulletins for mountaineers, the Sanskrit bulletin - and there could be more. We will have occasion to speak of them later in the book. Different audiences have different tastes and preferences and what, therefore, constitutes news for one is hardly that for another. The game of cricket is a striking example. It is played mainly in countries which- were once ruled by the British. So in many of the external bulletins of AIR, or the bulletins of other networks, cricket may not find a place even if the Indian team has scored a major victory. Some of the foreign languages have no word for cricket.

Even within India, there are regions which have much more interest in football or hockey. For example, the tribal people of eastern India and in the north-east of the country are excellent players of the games of football and hockey and are little interested in cricket.

This point has to be borne in mind by the editors compiling bulletins for such audiences.

EXERCISES:

1. Explain how audience interest decides the lead or headlines of a bulletin.
2. Why is it essential to repeat stories from a bulletin to another? How do you avoid giving the impression that you are repeating items already broadcast once or more?
3. What is the importance of a ten minute bulletin?

Chapter VIII

HOURLY BULLETINS AND SPECIAL BULLETINS

In today's fast moving world time never stands still. Things continue to happen and many of the events are newsworthy. Distances have been conquered. The world is a much smaller place than it was only a few years ago.

It goes without saying that the radio (as well as TV) must bring all such developments to the listeners without the least delay. The hourly bulletins came into being as an answer to this situation helping the listener to keep in touch. In the United States and some other countries these 'news on the hour' broadcasts came into vogue many years ago.

As we have seen in a previous chapter the news bulletin is part of a large programme. So when the media (radio and TV) are on the air for many hours of day and night there is scope, nay there is a need, also for news bulletins early in the morning and until late at night, in addition to those during the working hours and hours of relaxation.

From that to all-night programmes round the clock is the next step. The programmes naturally include bulletins.

In India, AIR introduced hourly bulletins in the seventies but since the radio was on the air only upto midnight (beginning from six in the morning) the last bulletin was also broadcast at midnight. During the Lok Sabha (lower house of Parliament) elections in March 1977 AIR broadcast for the first time hourly bulletins round the clock to bring the results to the listeners.

Interest in the elections and their results was high. The ruling Congress party had been challenged (and was actually ousted from power) by the Janata party which combined within itself all the non-communist opposition parties. The people had suffered a great deal in the 19 months preceding when an emergency had been in force.

The bulletins were heard with much avidity and there were many who kept awake until the wee hours of the morning to know the fate of many government ministers. The defeat of the incumbent Prime Minister, Mrs. Indira Gandhi, was announced at three a.m. on March 21. Crowds poured out into the streets during the hourly bulletin which carried the result. I happened to be the director of the News Services Division of AIR and those events are fresh in my mind.

Such heightened interest does not obtain in normal times. In any case, the regular hourly bulletins of AIR had to wait for at least ten more years before they could be scheduled. (The 1977 bulletins were a special occurrence.) The radio in India began putting out round-the-clock programmes and towards 1990 the hourly bulletins also became a regular feature.

Only a few people may be awake late at night or early in the morning and listen to the radio and your hourly bulletins. But since you are catering to them - people who are habitual late sleepers, those who may be driving and listening to their car radio, those who get up in the small hours of the morning and may switch on their sets - you have to ensure that they get the latest news, *plus* a brief roundup of the major, updated earlier stories.

The hourly bulletins have to be taken seriously, more seriously than they actually are. The issues involved in repeating stories and bearing in mind the needs of listeners who switch on from time to time or now and then to know the latest have been dealt with at some length in the previous chapter. The points made there have to be kept in mind by editors doing the hourly bulletins.

Whether it is the comparatively small number of listeners late at night and early in the morning or the fairly large number of listeners during the day and evening the editor has to approach his task as though there is a big audience waiting to listen. You cannot disappoint them by putting together a concotion of stories and offering it as an hourly bulletin. The hourly bulletin is as important, from the point of view of the listener as well as the broadcasting organization, as the major ten minute bulletins broadcast in the morning and evening series.

You must strive to make them newsy and not deny the listener any major story under the mistaken impression that such and such an item has been carried in a couple of earlier bulletins and can, therefore, be dropped from yours. The criteria, as always, must be: What is the news of the moment. Stories which have dated can be weeded out but those which are still valid have to be briefly touched upon in the five minute bulletin.

Also you have to note that your five minute hourly bulletin has no headlines and no repeating of the main points at the end. The bulletin must, therefore, contain all that is interesting and relevant on the hour but also be presented in such a manner that the listener gets to know, in a nutshell, everything worth knowing. Normally the listeners of the hourly bulletin are (a) those who are listening to some programmes or the other and would get to hear-your bulletin and (b) those who specially switch on their sets for the news on the hour.

In these days when the TV is offering you stiff competition you have to remember that the hourly bulletins help you to bring the audience back to the radio, if only for the duration of the bulletin. The TV does not have so many bulletins, certainly not news on the hour, and cannot compete with the radio in bringing news instantly.

We have gone into all this at some length because the practising editors often tend to take the hourly bulletins less seriously than they should. Remember that among the audience of these bulletins are professional men and women of your own fraternity who regularly switch on their transistors to find out about an anticipated development or just to know if there is anything that they should follow up.

Each hourly bulletin must be done as an individual offering of your organisation just as a diner expects that his order in the restaurant where he is eating is being individually attended to. The mass communication character of the newscast makes some difference and the interest evinced by a number of listeners would, of course be, common to many of them. But you have to remember that the radio (or TV) always says "we now bring *you* ... not *"all of you"*, the news or this or that programme.

Coming to the second part of this chapter, we have to note that the radio caters not only to the general listener but also to special audiences like women, the youth, farmers, the armed forces, industrial workers and the like. There can be and there often are special bulletins of interest to these sectional audiences, on a day-to-day basis, like the "Yuvavani" youth programmes of AIR, or there can be weekly and periodical news bulletins, as for the farmers in Doordarshan, the Indian TV-network.

Here we have to recall what we have learnt about the needs, tastes and preferences of different audiences. The youth bulletins should cover some national and foreign news as well as activities in which the youth are more interested like sports at home and abroad, news about educational activities and colleges and universities, employment programmes and so on.

Such stories may be available in the Pool itself and sometimes you have to look for them direct in the main sources also.

Stories for the special bulletins are not easily, in any case, not readily available. News agencies and the others bringing "News" to you are basically oriented towards politics. The government publicity organisations think their main task is to "project" the government and its ministers, not the various activities and programmes of the government.

Material relevant to the sectional audiences may not, therefore, just be there. You have to look hard for it. A special kind of nose for such news should be cultivated to locate the news.

This also goes for a peculiar kind of bulletin which AIR puts out and which may have its counterparts in other organisations. This is the Human Interest bulletin broadcast by AIR in Hindi and the other major Indian languages. (It is not broadcast in English, although the script for the non-Hindi bulletins is prepared in the GNR in English.)

Agencies hardly ever creed a story which answers the requirements of this special bulletin - stories which are off the beaten track, stories about human beings, their follies, kindness and val our, sacrifice and the urge to be good, stories which may make you laugh or imbibe a lesson. Pages of newspapers have to be closely scrutinised for such stories and the reporters asked to look for them in the course of their daily coverage.

For the sports bulletins and their likes, however, there is no dearth of news material. Such bulletins are generally scheduled in the evening hours by which time the results of many important events and tournaments, at home and in the international sphere, are available. The bulletins can thus be made really newsy.

Sports is one subject in which the listeners of all ages are interested and regrettably the editors are not much interested, not to the extent that they would willingly come forward to do them with some degree of excellence. This deficiency has to be made good since, as we shall see in a later chapter, sports is of prime importance in news.

There are some other types of special bulletins like the weather bulletins broadcast by AIR for the benefit of the mountaineers. Climbers who are up in the high mountains need a complete and daily dope on the weather prevailing in their region and how it would turn out to be in the next twenty-four hours.

The weather forecasting people come to their help and with the active involvement of the broadcast media a bulletin is put out only for the sake of the various expeditions. The bulletin begins by saying as much: This special bulletin is broadcast for such-and-such expedition. It also indicates when the next bulletin will be broadcast and on what frequencies.

Years ago AIR had a special world affairs bulletin in which only international news was featured. This had a good reception in the beginning because, as we have noted, the evening bulletins are usually full of home stories and the world news get a place only if it is of great significance.

However, the interest in this special bulletin gradually began to fade, partly because, news cannot be parcelled and any bulletin should have a home content to be of interest to the listeners.

Mention must be made here of a peculiar bulletin broadcast by AIR - the Sanskrit bulletin which goes on the air every morning and evening. Many people have not been able to grasp the purpose of a daily bulletin in a classical language and some have even objected to it. But there is a special background which must be grasped.

The external services of the German radio organisation was found to be broadcasting a weekly news bulletin in Sanskrit even before AIR introduced its daily morning bulletin in the language in 1974. (The second bulletin in the evening, which was unnecessary, was added during the Emergency, one of the excesses of that period.) The Germans did their weekly programme to show how much they cared for a language which a number of eminent Sanskrit scholars from that nation have studied and to which they have contributed in great measure, Maxmueller and the others.

The radio network in India, on the other hand, had a number of Sanskrit programmes like plays and recitations on and off but nothing in the nature of a daily programme in a language which has enriched most Indian languages and which holds the most precious heritage of India. A daily bulletin was seen as an answer to this felt need because it would be easy to follow as the news would be known to many listeners.

Nobody was under any illusion that listeners in any significant number, perhaps not even a handful, would derive their daily quota of news from the bulletin. It was conceived as a vehicle of carrying to the listener an interesting and easily understandable programme in Sanskrit from day to day.

It fell to my lot to implement an old decision to start this bulletin and with my close acquaintance with Sanskrit language and literature it became possible to lay the foundations of a programme which many Sanskrit lovers and the more knowledgeable among the listeners could follow from day to day. The language was specially prescribed to be simple but idiomatic and, the pronounciation chaste and palatable. Many listeners wrote to us to say how much they appreciated the daily bulletin and even now people express such sentiments.

The question is: what kind of stories should go into this bulletin. It is clear that since the bulletin was expected to be and is actually listened to for the pleasure of hearing Sanskrit being spoken rather than as a source of news the stories should be simple, known items of news which the listeners may have already heard in the respective languages or in English. In addition the bulletin should have stories which are of cultural significance, stories relating to education is general and, of course, those about Sanskrit itself.

Some people have raised the issue whether this broadcast does not take away from the time which should be devoted to news bulletins in the spoken languages. This question is based on a misunderstanding since AIR has covered all languages and even the tribal dialects in its daily news schedule. Sanskrit programmes have, on the other hand, a steady following and providing a bulletin in that language would not come in the way of any language while giving Sanskrit lovers something interesting from day to day.

As we have seen, sports and such other special bulletins command a large following while human interest bulletins and Sanskrit serve a limited audience. The special weather bulletins are designed to help a group of people and others would hardly be interested in them even if they heard it.

EXERCISES:

1. Make a human interest bulletin of five minutes from interesting reports in the daily press.
2. How are the special bulletins different from the general news bulletins?
3. What is the significance of the hourly bulletins now that TV programmes are available to the audience for most of the day and night?

Chapter IX

HEADLINES

We have already spoken about headlines in an earlier chapter. Their role is to give the listener a glimpse of what your bulletin offers just like a newspaper tells its readers in the heading of a story what the story may hold for him. The heading can only give you a brief insight into the long story which it heads.

Likewise, a radio bulletin gives only an indication of what the bulletin as a whole and its main stories offer. The headline have to be brief, crisp and striking short sentences which means you cannot cram too much information into them. They are, as we said earlier, like the dressing of a shop window which seeks to attract the shoppers to step in and buy something.

The headline must not reveal much. To cover many points of a story the headline will have to be long and perhaps consist of two or three sentences which is not correct. For, if you tell the listener most of what your story is going to offer what is left for you to say in the story itself?

The headline reveals something but not too much. It must reveal enough to attract the audience to wait for the main body of the bulletin which would then satisfy his curiosity which your headlines are supposed to have aroused.

To enable the main bulletin to cover as many items as possible you have to limit the number of headlines.

Remember that the headlines are going to be repeated at the end of your bulletin. Along with the repetition, the headlines should not take away more than about 60 to 70 words of your bulletin, if it is a ten minute bulletin you are writing.

This means that the ten minute bulletin can have no more than four headlines and a fifteen minute newscast can have five headlines. This number can be slightly increased, say by a single headline in each case, if you have a major story which needs two headlines. As we have seen, stories of great national significance or even an international story having several aspects may require a second headline. In that case, if you can limit yourself to two other headlines you can still be within the norm. But if you must exceed the four headline limit, do it only by adding a headline and no more.

There are both considerations to be kept in mind - the need to minimise the overall wordage of headlines and the requirement that a headline itself must be succinct and crisp.

Normally the brevity of the headline can be achieved by not including more than a single point in it. Look at the following headlines:

Mount Everest has been climbed.

Jawaharlal Nehru has passed away.

Rajiv Gandhi has been killed in a suspected LTTE human bomb attack.

Leander Paes has won the US Open Juniors title.

Mohun Bagan have lifted the Durand Trophy again.

Narasimha Rao has been elected leader of the Congress (I) party in Parliament.

You must have noticed that there are no more than twelve words in any of the headlines. One or two have only five words and yet all of them have been able to convey a lot to the listener, enough to make him sit up and take notice of your bulletin and wait for the main body of the news.

The first two were actually used as headlines. When Everest was climbed, popularly referred to as "conquered" and Edmund Hillary and Tensing Norgay set foot on the world's highest mountain, being the first human beings to do so, it was a major story. The Everest expedition led by Britain's John Hunt, of which Hillary and Tensing were members, was then much in the news. The listener interest was intense and when the expedition succeeded in its mission, the brief headline was able to break the news and convey a great deal.

The story about the killing of Rajiv Gandhi was on a different footing. He was actually on an election campaign and a brief headline "Rajiv Gandhi has been killed" would, no doubt, have conveyed much but there would still be gnawing deficiencies. How was a man suddenly killed when he was engaged in, a democratic persuasion process?

A bit of information has to be added to satisfy the listener. The manner of killing which was a novelty because this type of terrorist killing had not been used before in India by any group had to be brought out. What is equally important, by identifying a suspected group you are removing the suspicion from other terrorist groups. This had to be done in the headline itself because many people would start reacting after listening to the headline.

The shorter a headline the more interesting and striking it is. By saving a few words in each headline and its repetition you can cover one more news item.

Each of these sample headlines is able to reveal something useful and interesting and yet keep the listener on his toes to take in your bulletin. The headline should, however, never be vague, making the listener fume and fret because you have told him nothing. Like saying “India is struggling at Cape Town” instead of saying “India have lost four wickets for only sixty in the Cape Town test”.

The fact that you should not say more than what is enough to arouse the listener’s interest does not mean that you have to be delightfully vague. A headline must say something of significance, something which is newsy. “India struggling” gives some information but it is hardly informative enough to satisfy some curiosity of the listener. In fact, the headline shows that the editor has not taken any pains at all to extract a good headline out of the story.

As we explained in the early part of the book, the editor must go on drafting the headlines while he is writing his bulletin. More than the required number of headlines should be drafted and you should go on polishing them until you are yourself satisfied about their quality and ability to fulfil the norms we have explained. Out of say six drafted headlines you can finally select the required four. If you are doing a fifteen minute bulletin you should have drafted seven different headlines and then finally you choose five, along with the lead stories of different bunches.

Generally the first sentence, the lead of the headline item, would yield the headline also. But you should take care not to reproduce the exact first sentence in the headline. Variation between the story’s lead and the headline is necessary. If the lead is “the government today appointed a commission of inquiry headed by a judge of the Allahabad high court to inquire into the Ayodhya incident”, you can say in the headline “a commission of inquiry has been set up to probe the Ayodhya incident”.

Specially if the story is also the lead of your bulletin the variation becomes essential because the story is going to be read out. soon after the headlines have been broadcast. If for some reason the lead of your story has not been brought out correctly in the first sentence your must make good the omission in the headlines.

Apart from the lead story being taken first in the first bunch you have to take the third or fourth headline story at the start of the second bunch (in a ten-minute bulletin). The point made here is that the bunch must open with a more newsy item.

If you have headlined a sports story you ought to ensure that the story is not crowded out. For a broadcaster it is unpardonable to headline a story and not broadcast the item itself and allow it to be crowded out. As we saw in the chapter on compiling of bulletins the crowding out is a matter for internal information only. For the listener the item is just not there.

Finally a word about the practice that has recently come into vogue of giving newspaper heading-type headlines to radio and TV bulletins. That is, these headlines are incomplete sentences like headings in the daily press - like "five communal organisations banned", instead of "five communal organisations have been banned." The tendency is to say: "The Prime Minister says peace and tranquillity will be restored soon" when the headlines could easily have said, as we should do: "The Prime Minister has said peace and .. "

A radio and TV newscast must not carry a heading and beguile the listener into believing it is a headline. You must have seen that even from the point of economy of words and shortness of sentences the samples we have given in this chapter earlier are full sentences.

When AIR introduced the special sports bulletin in 1974 snappy heading-type headlines were used. This was done because for one thing there were headlines in the bulletin even though it was (and continues to be) a five minute bulletin. You can headline items and focus on three different stories and sports and yet not waste too many words on the headlines. Secondly, in sports bulletins a little bit of snappiness is permissible, just as in the writing of sports stories we allow the editor to use flowery and striking words and phrases, like a "glorious shot" "a spectacular goal" "a samshing hit" and so on. Normally such adjectives and attributes would be excluded from news items.

But to extend this type of ear-catching headlines to normal radio and TV bulletins is not good broadcasting. It would, therefore, be better to employ complete sentences in the headlines of the two media as was the case until some years ago. In the TV medium the facility of captions is available and these can as well convey full sentences as they can in the shorter headline-like headings.

EXERCISES:

1. Try to improve the headlines of the bulletin we have reproduced in an earlier chapter.
2. Why is it inadvisable to give a large number of headlines to a radio/TV newscast?
3. A headline is like a display in a shop window. Comment.

Chapter X

EXTERNAL BULLETINS

Every major broadcasting organisation (and some small ones too) have an external component in their programmes. The BBC is not .the only one to have extensive radio programmes for listeners abroad. The BBC's external services are entirely financed by the British Foreign Office. The American law does not permit the government to beam any radio or TV programmes to audiences at home. But the United States has a major set-up to broadcast programmes to listeners abroad - through the instrumentality of the Voice of America.

The External Services of AIR were actually started when the organisation was part of a foreign government's propaganda machine during British rule over India. During the second world war Britain found the external arm of Indian broadcasting very useful in projecting its views to audiences under Japanese occupation in China and the entire east and south Asia (then called the Far East, because it was the farthest from the western hemisphere.)

After independence the External Services were found equally, if not more, useful by free India's government. For example, the newly started Indonesian service (in 1949) was the only friendly broadcasting medium for the Indonesians who then were under Dutch occupation and all their national leaders were under detention. The news bulletins in the Indonesian language as, well as the daily commentary (which I happened to write for a long time) were avidly listened to by Indonesian radio users.

Likewise, the Burmese services of AIR and some of the other external services had a sizable audience. Naturally changes came about in the broadcasting field and in the world at large. The new medium of television has taken away much of the audience of radio. Consequently listening to the radio has declined everywhere. As a result of these changes the external broadcasts have lost a substantial part of their earlier importance. All the same, policy makers continue to hold that external broadcasts specifically directed to foreign audiences are still valid and useful.

Through its external broadcasts every country seeks to project itself to the foreign audiences, promote closer relations with the people there and put across its point of view on national issues and international affairs.

As we have noted earlier, all broadcast programmes have a news component as a matter of the daily schedule. Normally, therefore, all external broadcasts consist of a mixture of different items, including news, views in the form of commentaries, coverage of actual events like a major international event taking place in the country of origin, skits, drama, features and music. The last item may be both the music of the country to which you are broadcasting, some widely popular music, like the pop variety of relevance to the listeners and, to the extent possible, some music of the country of origin of the broadcast.

Every news bulletin, as we have noted more than once, must cover the news of the moment and that applies to an external bulletin. It is possible the audience has already had some exposure to a few of the items. But that does not matter while you are framing your bulletin. For example, let us suppose you are broadcasting a bulletin in your external services to Indonesia and that country is going through an election to choose a new parliament. The listener must have heard some news about the poll and if the results have started coming in he may have got some information about that too.

But when you beam a news bulletin to that country you must also put the listener wise about the results and the election campaign. It may be your coverage is more objective and well rounded and may, for that reason, be all the more welcome to the audience. Your bulletin will also cover other news of the region of south east Asia, the rest of the world and about India, or the country of origin, whichever it is.

Thus your coverage must be complete in the sense that news which is relevant must not be excluded and it could also turn out to be more objective than the national station or stations may be able to offer.

The contents of an external bulletin should be somewhat as follows:

(a) World news and news of that region: (b) news from and about the country to which you are broadcasting; and (c) news from your own country.

The bulletin has to be a judicious and balanced mixture of all three components, reflecting the major stories of that hour. You must, of course, coverback on the developments since your last bulletin in that particular cycle, since the last morning bulletin if you are broadcasting in the evening, or a twenty-four hour coverback if there is only one news bulletin in a day. The coverback aspect, must, however not be overstressed and "old" stories need not be included just for the sake of it. Such stories can be ignored or redrafted to include new points which can then form the lead of the item.

The external broadcasts themselves can be sub-divided into three broad categories. Taking AIR's external bulletins into account we have to note that AIR broadcasts in a number of Indian languages - Hindi, Gujarati, Tamil, Bengali, for example - in its external services. The Indian network also has 'a General Overseas Service (GOS) in English which is on the air for several hours. This service is beamed to a number of English knowing countries, in Asia, Africa, Australia and New Zealand; besides Europe. Finally, AIR has programmes in foreign languages like Arabic, Russian, French and so on.

The presentation of the news as well as the contents of the bulletins have to vary to a significant extent for the three kinds of audiences. The audience for the bulletins in the Indian languages is Indian or of Indian origin and may have some acquaintance with Indian names, values and beliefs and may have a continuous knowledge of developing Indian stories. It would naturally be more interested in things Indian than the other two types of audiences.

You can, therefore, cover more Indian stories in such bulletins and more details of such stories can also be included. At the same time you have to bear two points in mind. The first is that any bulletin, to be so called, must have all relevant news of the moment, whether it is news about India or the world outside. The second point, which is more important, is that the audiences of these bulletins may not be all that familiar with, Indian developments, although they are of Indian origin.

Another aspect of the second point made above is that some of the bulletins may actually be meant for people of another country although the language is one spoken in India. For example, Bengali is the language not only of the people of India's West Bengal state but it is also the language of the people of Bangladesh. Similarly the Urdu bulletins in-the External Services of AIR are primarily addressed to listeners in Pakistan, although Urdu is as much an Indian language as it is one of the main languages of Pakistan.

Even in the case of Gujarati or Tamil, the audiences of AIR's external newscasts, in Africa or South East Asia and Sri Lanka, may not be entirely familiar with Indian events and happenings. So, what is expected of you is that you would present the Indian stories in these bulletins with a little bit of background and explanation. In the other two categories - the GOS English bulletins and those in non-Indian languages - the "backgrounding" has to be done as a matter of routine.

If your story is about Nashik town in Maharashtra you have to say, "in Nashik, south of Bombay". Similarly you must say "in Amritsar, the city in India's Punjab state on the border with Pakistan". The unfamiliar has to be made familiar and the unknown made a little less so, if not entirely known, by suitable explanation and by adding background.

The background need not be too long. You can keep formulas ready. The Lok Sabha has to be always explained as "the lower house of Parliament". If the story is about the election of the leader of the majority party in the lower house of Parliament you must add: "This paves the way for Mr..... being asked to form a new government, as Prime Minister. The President, Dr Shanker Dayal Sharma, may swear in Mr... soon." You can, even say: "Mr... is to be the new Prime Minister of India. The formality of his being sworn in is expected ... "

In other words, developments may be clear to the home audiences but to a foreign audience they have to be *made* clear. This example should help you to understand how most home stories have to be explained and their significance brought out for foreign listeners, apart from adding factual information wherever necessary. Any reference to India's five year plan - there would be many in some bulletins - would be required to be, elaborated by adding: "The eighth plan began in April 1992."

If there are demands by any responsible party or prominent leader for a mid-term poll you have to explain, if you are carrying the story in any external bulletin, that the present house was elected in June 1991 and elections, in the normal course, are due in June 1996. The significance of a mid-term poll may be clear to listeners at home - sometimes the home audiences may also appreciate a little background information but a foreign audience may be left utterly at a loss to understand why there is a call for a mid-term poll and what it all amounts to.

The editor doing a home story for an external bulletin is like a foreign correspondent reporting developments in India to his readers or listeners back home in his own country. The editor has to put himself in that position to be able to do justice to the stories, make the task of the foreign listener easy and also achieve the purpose of broadcasting to audiences abroad.

For "externalising" the home stories, sometimes AIR has under the editor-in-charge an external Pool. The idea is to help an editor in a hurry to have readymade items for his external bulletin just as the editor of a home bulletin has readymade Pool stories at his disposal. In any case, whether there is such Pool arrangement or not the duty of the external editor is to make the home stories understandable to his audience.

For organisations where the Pool system does not prevail, the editor has to render each home story in a manner which makes it easy for his listeners abroad to understand the importance of the story just as he has to prepare good radio news items from source material for his home audience.

The simple formula is: Will the story make sense to my listeners. Easy comprehension is our guide in all bulletins and the principle is the same for the external audience too.

There is also a connected point which we must consider here. Some editors are under the illusion that their task is to cover only "good" news from India or the country of origin of the bulletin. This is a wrong way to approach our task. News is neither good nor bad and any assumption that the foreign audience has no other access to the Indian news is misconceived.

Even in the old days, the foreign listener - even the most sympathetic one - had other sources of news. He could read his local papers and listen to his own national or local radio or listen to other foreign. stations. If he listens to your broadcasts it is not too much to believe that he also tune in to other stations. These stations are not always too friendly to your country.

Now, of course, the sources of information are many more. There is the spy-in-the-sky, the satellite broadcasts on TV from other countries and they can bring the "bad" news from your country to a foreign audience. So, you can rightly presume that a foreign listener is not entirely dependent on your bulletin for all the news. If you make it a point to give him "bad" as well as what you think is good news your credibility will be enhanced. The foreign audience may then think better of you and thereby you will also be able to put across your national point of view and also plug in a few "good" news items too.

News must never be treated as good or bad. The effort should be to present a balanced and objective as well as truthful picture. The home audience is not at your disposal.

You have to hold them and secure their attention by presenting them with the latest news in an easy-to-understand style. The foreign audience is even less, much less, at your disposal.

In fact, you are in a highly competitive market. If in some countries a foreign broadcasting organisation is widely heard and has great credibility it is not because of its inherent strength but your weakness. You have failed, as an organisation, to bring to your listeners the truthful picture of developments at home and so the audiences are turning to a foreign source.

The authorities in power are, of course, more responsible for this state of affairs than the mediamen because the former lay down what should and should not be conveyed to the audience at home. This "advice" is then followed by pusillanimous mediamen in all respects and in their foreign broadcasts too. The play-safe attitude of the media persons - both those who are in commanding positions and those who are the operational men and women - comes handy to the government.

EXERCISES:

1. Pick up a major home story from the newspapers or the agency teleprinter and render it as a news item for a foreign bulletin.
2. What are the main guidelines for doing an external bulletin?
3. How will you explain the unfamiliar things in your country to a foreign audience in your bulletin? Give examples.

Chapter XI

LOCAL NEWS

The concept of local news, relating to the developments within, a limited area and of interest to those who live there, has not yet caught on in the Asian region, particularly in South Asia and South East Asia. Actually a region has many regional and local contours and there is much scope for presenting news of interest to the limited audience of the specified area.

If you extend the concept to further restricted areas of the city and town or the district and block of villages you have some idea of how a local news bulletin can really be interesting and how it can serve the local community.

The reason for the comparative lack of local news bulletins lies partly in the fact that the. radio has generally been organised on a national scale in most of these countries. With the national structure of the radio also came the national news concept. Thus bulletins came to be prepared and broadcast from a central point, to be relayed by the various cities and towns, often referred to as provincial places.

The local news or regional news *(Pradeshik Samachar* as it is known in India) was a later development. The basic idea is that the national bulletins were too preoccupied with national and international events to do full justice to local or regional news. With the regions, called states in

India, becoming more and more important and, in fact, demands being made for more autonomy, the emphasis was also shifting to the regions and there was thus much scope for regional bulletins.

Regional news bulletins were first introduced in AIR in the fifties, some fifteen years after AIR's News Services Division came into being and the national news network began to function. As of now all the 25 states and practically all the seven Union territories have regional news units in the respective radio stations and some states have more than one news originating unit.

The arrangement was, however, loose for some years and while some units genuinely tried (and succeeded) in - putting out news bulletins which were regional in character, others only highlighted the local news while they covered major national stories and sometimes even foreign news. In other words, they were nothing but additional news bulletins in which some regional news was featured.

The reason for this state of affairs was mainly lack of local news sources and partially lethargy and a failure to understand the real significance of the regional character of the bulletins. The paucity of local news sources was largely mitigated over the years with the appointment of PTCs (part time correspondents) who were specifically told to file stories for regional news and only rarely for the Delhi bulletins ('national news'). The radio organisation now has some 250 PTCs covering a majority of the districts of India.

The regional news bulletin to justify its name must reflect the developments within the specified state or part of the state' to which the bulletin is addressed. The states have long become the focus of attention although there is a great deal of centralisation too. The activities of the state government concerned and the opposition parties in the state, the state assembly proceedings, cultural and educational activities inside the state and of interest to its people regional sports and the like would form the subject matter of the regional bulletins.

Regional news bulletins are broadcast in many countries and, as we have said before, there broadcasts are related to the local radio concept or at least the regional concept. In this the regional station has to cater to the local audience which is presumed to be more concerned with what happens in its region, as different from its interest in the developments concerning the nation as a whole or the world.

Every person is concerned with the shopping and marketing in his place of living, his city or town or the district or block. The prices prevailing there are of significance to him, although prices have a national or even, international complexion. Whether the schools and colleges are having a holiday or the examinations have been postponed or are being held on schedule are matter of regional significance. The national bulletins would hardly be bothered and in any case, have no place for such details, except when there is some trouble in the educational institutions.

This is a typical case of the regional character of the local bulletins. The employment situation in the region would be of greater interest to the listeners there and in other parts of the country. The same goes for ecology, agriculture, scientific exploration and so on.

The scope is rather more unlimited than limited. Only the sources have to be built up and tapped for news. In the local radio concept the main idea is that the local station, like the leading local daily newspaper, should become the focal point of keeping the community informed about everything that concerns it. The news bulletin, therefore, can assume a big responsibility.

As we saw in the first chapter, news which has proximity to the audience has greater relevance and acceptability. While the local bulletin has yet to take any shape, at least the regional bulletin, which has for its compass the region or state as a whole, has to make a success. Only some regional bulletins have fulfilled the role assigned to them.

The TV also has a number of regional news bulletins but these are even more like what we referred to as the main features of the regional bulletins at the beginning of this chapter - news bulletins with a great deal of national and international news with regional stories given a prominent place. They are not an exclusively regional bulletin. If only they look for and develop the sources of news and shed some of their inhibitions the regional bulletins can not only become much more relevant than they are today, fulfil their real role but also challenge the "national" news bulletins.

The Doordarshan bulletins of the originating stations just have a little splash of state news like the Chief Minister visiting a development project or "inaugurating" a conference or a visiting minister from Delhi doing about the same thing. This kind of coverage has its place but if that is the only coverage of a local character while so many things are happening all around, the listeners or viewers cannot be blamed for not attaching importance to your regional bulletins.

The regional bulletin has to become a totally different offering from the station originating it and not a pale shadow of the one relayed from the national capital. The local weather, for example, is of much greater relevance to the people than the national weather picture which is what the bulletin from the "national" news originating centre provides. It matters much less to the listeners in the remote parts of the country if there is a cold wave in the northern parts because they have never seen a real winter.

Whether it is going to rain in your area, whether it is going to be hotter than it already is or it will be a hit cooler are things which interest your local listeners. If you can answer these questions and do it from day to day their involvement in your bulletins is going to grow.

As we said earlier, some of the inhibitions have to be given up. Crime, for example, is generally excluded from the purview of the radio-TV bulletins. That may not be bad but there is no reason why a big crime, a major bank robbery or the hunt for a killer at large should not be covered. The proceedings of a court trial of much interest to the people may not be covered from day to day but the judgment and the sentence would be a suitable subject for the radio/TV bulletins. At that time the main points of the case can be briefly presented.

Crimes with a social aspect, like the killings of young brides for extracting more dowry from their parents, would be a fit subject for coverage. The cases which result in sentence for the perpetrators of such crimes must also be covered. This list can be elaborated considerably. The important point to be noted is that while crime could continue to be taboo there are exceptions to the rule and there is much scope for expanding your news coverage and making the bulletins more interesting, without making them sensational or pandering to any base tastes.

The complaint of lack of news for the regional bulletins arises from lack of effort to cultivate and build up the sources and from an improper understanding of the character of the regional newscasts. It is also related to the inbuilt habit of highlighting the activities of the state bigwigs and limiting your vision to a narrow framework of VIP coverage.

Of course, the bulletins must not become the vehicle for

carrying stories which are hardly news in the name of expanding the regional character of the news. The local boss of an AIR station wanted the regional bulletin to cover all literary meetings over which he was invited to preside. Even ignoring the fact that such invitations were "arranged", on the understanding that the proceedings would be reported in the news, this kind of coverage can only make the bulletin lose its credibility.

There was, on the other hand, a station head who would not permit the visit of a cinema personality to the town from where the news bulletin was originated. He applied the rigid code that the actor would gain in his commercial standing by getting such coverage. This was not only far-fetched, since the bulletin was heard only in a strictly limited area, but also short-sighted and supercilious because the regional bulletin was sought to be deprived of a rare coverage since the place was hardly ever visited by such interesting persons.

So, as always, a proper balance has to be struck and while excluding stories which are non-news and not allowing your bulletin to be used for projecting anybody you should not exclude news which has significance and holds interest for your listeners. If you look around you will find there is so much doing in your state and there is so much to report for you. Once you began to cover stories of relevance, your correspondents will take notice and themselves file more and more of them without your having to ask them to do so.

Again and again, we have to stress that the radio can become more relevant to the community and hold its own against the TV provided you make the bulletin more interesting. The regional bulletin is a major offering of the station and if it sets the pace and leads the way other programmes can also become more interesting to the audience and the radio can continue to make an impact.

It goes without saying that the sources of news have to be developed and . guided to cater to your requirements. The main sources, as we have seen, are the (1) news agencies; (2) your own reporters; and (3) handouts tendered at the newsdesk of the regional news unit.

The agencies have to be told, from time to time, to file stories from within your state or region, to suit your requirements and in time for your broadcast schedule. The agencies should know the schedule and ensure that a story of relevance is brought to you before the news bulletin is broadcast and not after the broadcast. If there is more than one agency in the field you should encourage competition between them. Occasionally, just for this purpose, you can quote an agency, so that the other is motivated not to miss such an item and the first one is strengthened in its resolve to file more such stories.

Your own reporters are expected to know your requirements well and are also expected to function as the real and main source of news to you. But even they must be reminded from time to time that the reason for their being there is the bulletin and whatever they do must help to strengthen the bulletin and make it more popular. If a reporter has failed to meet the deadline he must be gently told so. If he persists in his bad habit he must be pulled up and shown no remorse.

The reporter must write his copy in such a manner that it . can, if required, go straight into the bulletin and be taken to the news broadcasting studio. If his copy is found deficient in that respect he must be told about it and asked to improve his work.

The handouts, on the other hand, are written either in the official jargon or in the political jargon of the parties and trade unions. A considerable amount of editing and rewriting would be needed before they can be found useful as source material. But every handout must be looked into carefully. Those which are just not news should be rejected but others which can yield some news should be carefully examined.

In the regional stations, more than in the national capital where the central newsroom would be located, the pressure on the newsroom to put out stories from political parties, literary and cultural bodies and some publicity hunting bodies and individuals is much greater. You have to weed out such chaff and separate it from the wheat of good material and also withstand pressures. Your capacity to stand up to pressures would be considerably enhanced if you set high standards for your bulletin.

For the regional news there is no foreign monitoring. But your national newsroom can render you much help by transmitting stories from the national capital which are of relevance to you but of no use to the main newsroom there. For example, in the two houses of Parliament there are answers to members' questions everyday that the houses are in session and these contain a great deal of information about the states.

A member would, for example, ask: What are the national highway projects in my state, what is their progress and when such and such a project would be completed. The central newsroom would hardly ever use this material. But if a story based on it is telexed to the regional bulletin an interesting news item would become available to the bulletin.

Likewise, the other regional centres can act as sources of news to a different regional centre if they care to file stories of relevance to the latter. Thus, if a cultural festival of one state is being organised in another the latter can have limited interest in the story but the former can have greater interest and if a story is fed to it can only be grateful. Inter-state sports meets are regularly organised and the performances of the competitors of different states can be transmitted to them. Outstanding performances can also be highlighted for their benefit if the state's athletes or players have done well.

The regional bulletin need not confine itself to the news about the region from within the region. Anything of interest to the region, the developments affecting the region but taking place outside it and so on are some of the items which must figure in these bulletins. Possibly, some bulletins are already covering such stories but definitely the main newsroom and the other regional units are not habituated to function as a source of news for a regional bulletin.

It is the habit of packing a regional bulletin with the doings of the local VIPs and bigwigs and with items of a routine nature - so-and-so minister today visited the thermal power project in a certain place and stressed the need for speeding up the work on the project - which make the bulletin dull and ineffective. The blame lies more with the editor and his outlook (or the lack of it) than with the tools. The complaint of lack of material is hardly justified.

EXERCISES:

1. What are the points of difference between the national news bulletin and the regional one?
2. Write a note on the importance of local radio and how it can serve the local community.
3. What will you do to make your regional news bulletin more interesting and relevant to the audience?

Chapter XII

REPORTING FOR THE RADIO

We have seen that the reporter's stories form an important part of a news bulletin. This source of news is of special importance because the reporter is part and parcel of your organisation and is fully aware of your requirements as well as the spoken word style of writing. He is accustomed to check and double check the facts of his story.

The agency story may need to be further checked sometimes but when your reporter brings you a story you can take it with full confidence in the facts and his presentation of them.

It has been mentioned more than once in the previous pages that the reporter's copy is expected to be so good that it can, if the time factor so demands, be taken straight to the studio where a newsreader is about to start reading a bulletin or is actually in the midst of it. The reporter is a trained broadcast journalist.

In several organisations it is the practice to assign all freshers to the newsroom where they pick up or improve the basics of news writing, imbibe the discipline and the drill of broadcasting, learn how to compile bulletins and, what is equally important, know the significance of the reporter's role.

Only after this grounding is a promising editor chosen to join the reporting team. Sometimes it may also happen that a broadcast journalist may be chosen almost on the morrow of his entering the organisation to undertake reporting work. Even then he must spend some time with the newsroom and observe how the newswriting and bulletin compilation operations are conducted.

For those who have received basic training in broadcast journalism in a school of journalism or mass communication reporting is part of his training. He is taught to edit and write the news and is also trained in reporting assignments, But he has also got to pick up many things while he is working on the job.

The broadcast journalist has to learn to use the tape recorder and his voice in reporting. He may be called upon to do voiced despatches for the bulletins and for the newsreels and other programmes. Training of the voice is thus essential. This aspect is dealt with in a later chapter.

Here the important aspects of reporting for the electronic media are examined from the point of view of making the reporter an important element in the newscast. A good reporter must thus have:

(1) The ability to present news in the radio style, using simple language, short sentences, familiar words, in short, writing his story as though he was doing an item for the bulletin;

(2) Speed in drafting his story so as to lose the minimum time between the occurrence of an event and its coverage on the radio;

(3) Full regard for accuracy and truthfulness; and

(4) Complete understanding of the reporting drill including the arrangement for transport, telephone, telex or other telecommunication facilities, the objective always being to catch the next available bulletin.

It goes without saying that to be a successful reporter you must build up your sources of news. The scope for scoops, that is reporting exclusive stories, ahead of anyone else, is limited on the radio. This is for the simple reason that once a story is carried by a bulletin it is heard by your rivals and they can get on to it and report it in the very next day's newspapers while other broadcasting reporters can pick up your story for their bulletins later in the day.

But there is the classic case of the Swedish national radio which reported in April 1987 that bribes had been paid in the contract for supply of field guns for the Indian army by the Bofors company of Sweden. The contract was worth more than 14,000 million rupees. It was obtained by the Swedish manufacturers in the face of stiff competition from the French, Austrian and British suppliers. The story affected the course of Indian politics for a number of years and virtually cost Prime Minister Rajiv Gandhi his office in the general election of November 1989.

The Swedish radio story, however, became the property of the world media, specially the Indian media, within minutes of broadcast, although it brought the team which worked on the story great professional credit. Exclusive stories are thus possible to be done for the radio as much as for a newspaper but the life of the "exclusive" story is hardly a few hours, sometimes only a few minutes.

Such exclusive stories can be done if you cultivate the sources of information, follow the clues intelligently and have the ability to piece together different strands which ultimately go to make a story. Personal equation with the sources has to be established by continuous contacts and by demonstrating your ability to report a story accurately and secure good coverage for it in your media.

Contacts are essential even If you are not seeking an exclusive story. Suppose a briefing of an important development is scheduled for 5-30 p.m. and you have an important bulletin in your organisation scheduled for 6 p.m. Your close relations with the source would help you to ensure that the briefing is not delayed and you are able to get out of the briefing room some minutes before the 6 p.m. news is to go on the air so that the main points are reported. All this would be possible only if the source and you had a good rapport. He would then keep your requirements in mind.

The use of the telephone as a means of fast communication is of special importance in the instant medium of the radio. The reporter must thus be able to talk to the source direct on phone, get confirmation or denial of stories the reporter may have received from other sources but about whose authenticity there is some doubt, get a few highlights of a story for an early bulletin while the details would be covered in a later, bigger bulletin and even get the intimation of briefing well in time.

Spokespersons are not very prompt or meticulous in informing the media of likely stories expected to break and sometimes may forget or neglect to inform you of a major, last-minute briefing or press conference. The reporter has, therefore, to have good personal relations with the source. Contacts must also be built up at higher levels so that you know what is going on and the knowledge of undercurrents which often precede a major development may keep you and your organisation in readiness to face the story when it does land.

Even if your organisation has no use for speculative stories it is important to know the trends and the forces at work which may influence the final decision. Your alertness and continuous contacts would also help you and your network to steer clear of stories which are planted by different groups and sometimes even by the government.

The reporter must inspire confidence among his

editors. This is essential because the newsroom is bombarded with stories and reports and some of them may be totally without foundation. The reporter has to advise the editors about them and has thus to act as the eyes and ears of his organisation and put the newsroom wise about political or even major economic stories.

Of course, the editors should come to their own conclusions and need not lean on the reporter all the time. Suppose the newsroom receives, from the news agencies or from other some source, a story saying some of the ruling party's key figures are likely to quit the party and may precipitate a crisis for the government. If true, the story is highly significant but your reporter must first be asked to check on it, before the next bulletin is to go on the air.

Now even the reporter could go wrong. He, for example, could be misled by a source he has found otherwise dependable and trustworthy. The source may even be ignorant and to hide his ignorance may flatly deny the story. So, you must seek confirmation from another source. The story cannot just be spiked, that is rejected, simply because your reporter says it should be.

Two examples will make this point clear. Years ago, we received in the AIR newsroom a report saying the then finance minister, a confirmed widower, had married a political leader who was a widow. The news agency had not quoted the source for the story, which it should have done. So, we had to ask the finance minister himself and he was not only available but willing to confirm the story.

In 1977, on the eve of the general election, Jagjivan Ram, the virtual No.2 in Mrs. Gandhi's cabinet and the Congress party, resigned from the government and the party, alongwith a few others of some consequence. This was the time when the Janata party had been challenging Mrs. Gandhi (and eventually won the election too).

There was some time between the receipt of the report and the next scheduled bulletin. We asked a senior reporter to rush to Jagjivan Ram's house and he found the elderly leader surrounded by his followers. The leader willingly gave the reporter a copy of his statement on his "defection". The story of his resignation was carried by us in the next available bulletin after proper confirmation.

The reporter's good contacts with the resigning or "defecting" leaders helped us to obtain the needed confirmation. We could have carried the story - perhaps we would have - quoting the agency as the source even if the confirmation part would have been waived. In any case, within hours the ruling party had also reacted thus lending credibility to the resignations. The only question could be whether we should have waited that long. We did not.

The four essential requirements of the mental makeup and training of a reporter of the radio, as outlined earlier in this chapter, have to be fully grasped. The reporter must be able to convey whatever he has gathered, in a summarised form suitable to the radio. The story drafted by him should be a finished product. While the Pool (where it exists) and the bulletin editor may subject it to some amount of rewriting and polishing his effort must be to present a story as neat and finished as possible.

The reporter must be fully aware of the schedule of the bulletins so that he is able to catch the next available newscast after he has gathered the facts and done a story. If the reporter has taken that - trouble he will find that his story lands in the newsroom well before the agency or agencies begin to creed theirs. Every organisation prefers to take and highlight its own correspondent's story but the reporter should also be fast and strive to be ahead of the agencies.

He has to note that the details of a story can wait but not the news. He must, therefore, telephone the newsroom or hand in a typed story, if he is at hand, to give the highlights of a story. He can then sit down and do a detailed and revised version which would naturally replace the first rush version.

It is here that advance preparations for lining up telephone or other telecommunications facilities and being aware of the needs of different bulletins are important. Sometimes a draft story could be held in readiness and filed as soon as the event takes place as expected. But here caution is necessary.

In 1975, the then railway minister was to start work formally on an important project in Bihar and he was scheduled to make a speech before it, as is the custom. One of the national news agencies which had been given a copy of his speech went ahead and said the event took place, gave a few points from the speech and did not bother even to attach the conventional warning "check against delivery" or "use after the speech has actually been delivered."

The railway minister, as it happened, was late and the opening ceremony was not performed even as we in AIR broadcast the story of his having done it and covered points of his speech. What was worse, the minister was the victim of a grenade attack, the speech was never delivered and, in fact, he died the next day. The agency, jumping the embargo on the release of the speech by the railway PRO and not even observing the caution of saying confirmation on, the opening ceremony be awaited had caused AIR a great deal of embarrassment.

But if you have obtained a copy of a major speech in

advance and file your story after obtaining the confirmation of its delivery you can steal a march over your rivals and give your listeners a story ahead of all others.

Facts must, however, be checked and in the race for being first they must never be trifled with or ignored. The radio medium has more credibility than the printed word which, in any case, takes considerably more time to appear. But credibility is a brittle thing and may be lost by a grave error or two.

Speculative stories have to be taken with a pinch of salt but they cannot be shunned altogether. Your experience and contacts would tell you how much truth these stories, received often from the agencies, have. You have to guide the newsroom on that score.

The importance of writing a story in the spoken word style cannot be overemphasised. If you do justice to your draft it would not only find a place of honour in the finished bulletin but you would also earn a reputation for turning out good copy. Such reporters are treated with respect by the editors and their stories are awaited. Your story replaces the agency version the moment your draft comes in. It is up to you to maintain your reputation.

The drafting must be done carefully even while you beat the various deadlines. Practice is required so that when you sit down to type your story the language and the words would flow automatically from you and everything would fall in place.

As we have seen before, the source must be approached to check the facts but you must not be squeamish and allow yourself to be bullied by a source which would like to keep out all unpleasant points of a story. While the source may be quoted for his version you may also get the details from the relevant people and place their version side by side.

For example, you may say: "The police claimed that the 'bandh' (work stoppage) called by the Indian Workers party failed to evoke any response. But the chairman of the party said it was a success. While banks were open and some government offices had partial attendance most of the shops and factories were closed and public transport was working fitfully." You need not be content with just carrying the police version which was, in this case, apparently doctored.

On occasions, however, the police would be the main source. Like crime or communal rioting which has a sensitive aspect to it and your stories may have widespread repercussions. The police version in such cases would be important but you need not feel tied hand and foot, if the facts as you can find out point to the contrary.

In December 1990, the district administration (police *plus* the civil authority) in Aligarh, in Uttar Pradesh state, announced that the Aligarh Muslim university had been closed and the students had been asked to vacate their hostels. This was during a period of communal violence. The story was used by AIR (and Doordarshan) following the district authorities' announcement.

Actually the Vice-Chancellor had not agreed to the district administration's suggestion for closing the university and the students vacating their hostels. This was a case in which the official version was not deliberately doctored but it was incorrect because the university was not actually closed.

The correct versions was that the district authorities had asked the university to close down but their suggestion had been turned down.

A nice balance has to be struck between the need to be first with the news and the checking of facts. Before giving them wide coverage you have to make a decision based upon your experience, the guidelines which you have to follow and the need to keep the listeners informed.

There is a case of the report monitored by AIR's Shimla monitoring organisation in July 1977 from Radio Pakistan's Urdu bulletin early one morning. The bulletin carried a story, without a headline and without any other importance given to it, saying the armed forces of the country were concerned about instability in Pakistan and had come to the conclusion that they must take the reins of the government in their hands.

Except this brief story there was no other indication that the armed forces of Pakistan had struck once again and deposed the government (of Prime Minister Zulfiqar Ali Bhutto). As soon as the monitor alerted the newsroom in Delhi we took stock of the story, looked for any other indication from a different source or from the radio itself, but in vain.

Time was running out as the 0800 hours Hindi and 0810 English bulletins were to go on the air within less than half an hour. We weighed all the factors and facts available (I was then Detector of the News Services Division of AIR) and decided we would use the story and say there was a military coup in Pakistan. As soon as the bulletins went on the air, we were quoted by the world media which picked up the story from AIR. The story turned out to be a hundred per cent correct. Bhutto had, in fact, been ousted from power by the military which had installed Gen. Zia-ul-Huq as his successor.

We could have done the story with the same caution and circumspection with which the hedged-in version had been done by the source. But that would hardly have been a news item. Either the story of a coup was true and the Prime

Minister had lost power (the Pakistan radio story named no names) or it was not. Details began to flow as the day progressed and Islamabad naturally became the focal point of the developments.

This is a case in which a deliberately mystified version was read properly and the truth was brought out. The point made here, however, is valid in the daily chores of a reporter who has also to follow up clues and take a decision whether a story could be made out of the bits he has gathered and whether the bits fit in and his judgment is right.

EXERCISES:

1. What are the essentials of good radio reporting?
2. Write on the importance of checking facts while reporting a story without losing any time.
3. Cover an important event in your neighborhood and compare it with the version done by the radio bulletin.

Chapter XIII

COMMON ERRORS IN DRAFTING

All editors have to grasp the correct usage of English, become aware of the need to follow it and use the correct and appropriate words and avoid mistakes. We know that for most people in India and the neighboring countries in South and South-East Asia, English is not their mother tongue. This means that mistakes can occur. They occur even in the English speaking countries. But by continuous practice and effort one can master the usage and write correct, idiomatic and simple English.

A large majority of the errors occur in the use of the definite and indefinite articles or failure to use them, in the use of prepositions, the use of the singular and plural forms and in not knowing the correct meaning and significance of the words employed.

It is not the electronic media alone who need to be aware of and follow the correct usage. The English press, including some of the dailies with large circulations, have been lapsing into wrong usage, proofreading errors and errors of facts, apart from bias in reporting.

Take the following front-page story in the Delhi edition of the *Times of India,* (December 14, 1992), considered one of the leading Indian dailies and rated one of the best in the world:

"Babri Case Handed Over to CBI

The Times of India News Service

New Delhi, December 13: The Central Burearu of

Investigation (CBI) will investigate into the demolition of the Babri mosque at Ayodhya on December 6, government spokesman announced here today.

The decision was taken by the centre in consultation with the UP government and a case in this regard has already been registered at Ayodhya, the spokesman said.

Meanwhile the Cabinet Committee for Political Affairs (CCPA) today reviewed the situation arising out of the communal violence in different parts of the country.

The committee meeting was presided over by a slightly indisposed Mr Narasimha Rao, and other members including Mr Arjun Singh.

The committee reportedly expressed satisfaction over the law and order situation and discussed measures to step up relief measures."

Every paragraph in the story above has an error, more than one in some paragraphs. In the very first paragraph, the words investigation and investigate are repeated in close proximity. Then *"investigate into"* is not correct as the verb investigate does not take a preposition.

Furthermore in the same paragraph (and sentence), there is neither a definite nor an indefinite article before "government spokesman". It should be "a government spokesman" but even *"the* government spokesman" would be permissible, presuming there is only a single spokesman (actually there are more.)

Coming to the second paragraph a "case in this regard" is better written as a "criminal case on the demolition of the mosque".

In the third paragraph of the *Times of India* story, quoted above, the CCPA has been referred to as the Cabinet Committee *for* Political Affairs. But the correct way to write it is "the Cabinet Committee *on* Political Affairs," which is also the CCP A's name.

The second last para says the CCPA meeting was presided over "by a slightly indisposed Mr. Narasimha Rao and other members including Mr Arjun Singh." Are we to understand that not only a slightly indisposed Narasimha Rao but all its members, including Mr Arjun Singh, *presided* over the meeting which is what the sentence means?

Even the last paragraph is not free of error. The word "measures" is repeated in close proximity - "measures to step up relief measures."

Incorrect usage, loose drafting, unawareness of the finer points of writing and factual errors like the wrong name of the CCPA, in a story on the front page of the paper, do not create a good impression about the paper's concern for good writing. The example we have quoted above is also not an untypical occurrence.

Let us see how such carelessness has permeated other newspapers. In the *Indian Express* of Delhi of December 17, the opening paragraph of a story captioned "Easy-going Surat on Rough Turf After Riots" reads as follows:

"SURAT The easy-going Surat has been shaken out of his stupor by the explosion of communal violence in the textile city which has over the last few days shred apart the secular fabric."

How can Surat, the proper noun of a city in south Gujarat, be shaken out of *his* stupor? Obviously the word Surat should be replaced by Surati, meaning a resident of the city. That this is just not a proofreading error becomes clear when you read on and find the sentence has been clumsily written. This is further confirmed when you see the word "shred" used in the past tense. The past of shred is *shreded* not shred. The word is also not aptly used.

In the *Statesman* of Delhi dated December 16 the following sentence occurs in a story headlined "Howard's End to Open Film Festival":

"With a weak Festival Directorate with comparatively junior officers dominated by the bureaucrats of the I and B ministry, with politicians adding their interference, with a plethora of committees dogged by star values, chamchas and a familiar old guard which has served on some committees or other every year, things predictably remain the same."

To begin with, the heading is wrong. "Howard's End" is the name of a film from abroad and we are told that the festival will open with its screening. We wish while giving us such interesting information the sub-editor had also shown some regard for grammar. How can a film "open" a festival? The festival can be said to open with the film.

The sentence reproduced above is a good example of how a story should not be written, for the electronic or any other media. How does the weak Festival Directorate go *with* the words "dominated by the bureaucrats of the I and B Ministry".

Then we are told the politicians are "adding" their interference. Adding to what? As it is written, the meaning is not clear, although the intention seems to be to say that the politicians' interference is adding to the confusion or poor performance of the weak directorate. The plethora of committees is supposed to be dominated by both values and individuals in the form of "chamchas", (hangers-on) and an old guard.

The radio/TV news writers are also not immune from the kind of errors pointed out above. But if they practice the basic guidelines of broadcast journalism they would I at least save themselves from the confusion that long-winded sentences lead their writers into.

Let us begin with the errors caused by wrong use of the definite and indefinite articles. The correct usage has to be mastered by going back to the standard books on the subject, reference to the dictionary whenever a doubt arises about the meaning of a word and study of books which are good examples of English writing not the kind of passages quoted above.

All that can be said by way of a *general guideline* on the use of articles in English is that all nouns except proper nouns, like names of persons and places (with some exceptions) and abstract nouns, take an article. The correct approach ought to be for you to ask yourself whether a definite or indefinite article should be there or not and which of the two would be appropriate.

Take the word "curfew" as an instance. The media habitually use it without an indefinite article and sometimes drop even the definite article when the same curfew is referred to again. It is incorrect to say: "Curfew was imposed on the walled city of Delhi today following incidents of communal violence." You have to say: "*A* curfew was imposed on ..." When the time comes for it, say: "*The* curfew in the old city of Delhi was relaxed following..", not "curfew was relaxed... "

"The Prime Minister was running *a* temperature and could not attend a meeting of the CCPA..." not running temperature.

When you refer to the actions or pronouncements of a government, like the Indian government or the state government of West Bengal, always say, "*the* government ... ". Thus it would be correct to say: "*The* government today further liberalised imports" not "government today further... "

By convention certain nouns do not take any article. The Indian Parliament is one such but both its houses, the

Lok Sabha, the lower house, and the Rajya Sabha, the upper house or the Council of States, have to be preceded by the definite article. The Various state assemblies must also be preceded by the definite article.

Say *"the* West Bengal Assembly passed the state budget today." "In Madras today, *the* assembly adopted a motion... ". *"The* assembly of Madhya Pradesh state has been dissolved by the Centre."

(In India, 'Centre' stands for the Central government.)

Proper nouns do not take any article but there are exceptions. Newspapers generally are written with a definite article - *The Times of India, The Straits Times, The Frontier Post.*

Rivers have also to be given the definite article - the Ganga, the Mekong, the Indus, the Volga. Mountains are another groups where the proper noun is preceded by the definite article - the Himalayas, the Alps, the Hindukush.

Street names, however, do without the definite articles, Parliament Street, Bukit Timah Road, Serangoon Road, Mahatma Gandhi Road.

As a rule, consonants take the indefinite article *"a"* while vowels are preceded by "an". The exceptions are those words whose first letter may be a consonant but has a vowel sound, like "honorable" and, by contrast, the words which begin with a vowel but have to be given the indefinite article "a" because the vowel is pronounced like a consonant.

Examples are *"an* honorable member of Parliament", "a unique achievement" "a United Nations representative".

The determining factor is the sound of the first letter, something of which as a spoken word mediaman you should be more particularly aware. For example, the word UN has a consonant sound but when it is part of a word like UNCTAD it will emit a vowel sound. So, any reference to a report of the

UNCTAD will be preceded by the indefinite article. Like, "*an* UNCTAD grant for trade development...".

Before we go on to prepositions we have to refer to a number of transitive verbs which must be followed by their object.

The most common of these are: "inform", "tell", "assure", and "warn". The person or persons or groups which have been informed, told, assured or warned must be placed after the verb.

Everyday there are obituary notices (paid advertisements) in leading dailies which are the worst culprits in this regard. It is common for them to say: "With profound grief we inform the sad demise of our beloved father Mr Amar Nath," The advertisement should say: "... we inform our relatives and friends" or "...inform all concerned".

That the advertisement department dictates terms to the editorial is well known but here its grammatical errors are also emulated by the editorial and news pages. Thus it is not unusual to find a story in a leading daily "The Prime Minister informed that the prices would be brought down after the winter crop." Here the person/s or group informed must be mentioned after the verb. "The Prime Minister informed the Lok Sabha that the prices..."

"He told that" is the most common error in conversation and this mistake creeps into statements in Parliament and the speaches of the VIPs. The editors in the newsroom have to be vigilant and not let such errors find their way into the bulletins.

Tell, inform, assure and similar transitive verbs are required to be followed by the object. There are alternatives like "say" where the object need not be used. "The Prime Minister said that the prices of essential goods would be brought down." You can then say he was answering a question in the Lok Sabha today on the price situation.

Like these verbs of common occurrence prepositions of common occurrence are also wrongly used. It is not unusual to find a newspaper saying: "The opposition charged the government *of* ineffective handling of the law and order situation." It should really be charged *with*. It would be correct to say the government was accused *of* ineffective handling of the law and order situation.

Another word which is often followed by a wrong preposition is "agree". "The Speaker pointed out that the opposition had earlier agreed *for* a late sitting of the house." It should actually be the opposition had agreed *to* a late sitting. Agreement is generally followed by *on*. "Agreement was reached today between the striking pilots and the airlines management *on* ending the strike." "India and the World Bank have reached an agreement *on* the use of the loan of ... ".

A list of frequently occurring prepositions and their correct usage will be found at the end of the book.

Certain verbs do not take any preposition, although it is often found that such prepositions are used. Discuss, mention, stress, emphasise are among these verbs. Discuss and mention must be followed by the object, not by a preposition. It is incorrect to say, "The leaders discussed *about* the problem of reservation of jobs..." You have to say: "The leaders discussed the problem of..."

Likewise, you have to say, "the headmaster stressed the value of punctuality in his address to the morning assembly" "The Prime Minister emphaeised the need for maintaining good relations with India's neighbours. "Not, the headmaster stressed *on,* or the Prime Minister emphasised *on* the need.

When stress and emphasis are used as nouns they take a preposition. "The headmaster laid stress *on* the value..” The Prime Minister laid emphasis *on* the need for...”

These are some of the most frequently occurring wrong uses of prepositions to which we have drawn attention here. There are several other verbs and nouns which are mistakenly followed by wrong prepositions. You have to be careful about not allowing such errors to creep into your news writing.

The correct usage of the plural and singular forms must also be grasped. If human beings are referred to in a collective sense, like *a number* of people, *a group* of students or a group of members of Parliament the form must be plural. Thus, “a number of people *are* afflicted by the virus”, or “a group of members of the ruling party *are* agitated over not being taken into confidence.... ” Of course, the words number, group and similar other words are used in singular otherwise. The number of the disgruntled members is increasing everyday, or, the group *has* been holding meetings..

A team is, however, generally referred to in singular. The team of doctors sent down from Delhi to examine the aged freedom fighter *has* left for the capital. But in sports events where teams compete the participant is referred to in the plural.

“India *have* won five gold medals in the meet so far”. “South Africa *have* won the one-day series”. It would be incorrect to say: “The United States *has* defeated Switzerland in the Davis Cup Final” You must say “The United States *have* defeated.. ”

When you refer to “one of” several, the noun which follows must be in the plural. “He is one of the politicians whom you can trust.” “India is one of the countries which have contributed to the Africa Fund.”

Hundred is only a unit and so when you are referring to one hundred you have to say either *“one hundred”* or *“a hundred.*" Not "wheat prices have gone up by hundred rupees in the past two years", but "*a hundred* rupees". "Sachin Tendulkar scored a fine hundred", not fine hundred.

The term et cetera, or etc, should, as far possible not be used. You can say: "The articles on display are machine tools transport machinery, consumer goods, fruit juices *and other products.*" Not "The articles on display are machine tools, Transport machinery, consumer goods, fruit juices *etc. etc.*" Expressions like *so on, and the like,* should be used in place of *et cetera.*

If you are prefacing a list of articles or individuals with "*include*" there is no justification for using etc. or even so on. For example, "those who called on the President today included the governors of several states, the minister for non-conventional energy, boy scouts etc." is not correct. The reason is that "included" carries with it the sense that there were others besides those listed. "Those who called on the President included several governors, the minister *of* (not *for)* non-conventional energy, and boy scouts and girl guides."

Often people commit an error in using the expression "it is time" or "it is high time". The clause which follows it must be in the past tense. "It is time we forgot the past and *thought* of the future," not "it is time we *forget* the past and think of the future."

The use of the simple past tense in your story must be accompanied by the time when the event occurred. "The Prime Minister *said* in New Delhi *today* that India will honour its commitments to the United Nations." But if you do not use the time (in that sentence) you have to use the imperfect past. "The Prime Minister *has said* India will honour its commitments to the United Nations."

In such a case, the place also cannot be mentioned. Like the time it must come in the next or subsequent sentence.

Adjectives in the bulletins must be sparingly used, except in sports stories where you should use them with abandon. "The Defence Minister made an effective rebuttal of the opposition's arguments," can be better written as "The Defence Minister rebutted the opposition's arguments." Rebutted itself means rebutted effectively.

People are not to be referred to as *"famous"*, *"renowned"* or even *"well known"*. In most cases, the word to be used is *"noted"*. "The noted Hindustani vocalist, Ustad..., has been honoured by the Sangeet Natak Akademi (the national academy of music and dance)".

Words like famous or outstanding should be reserved for outstanding personalities like Satyajit Ray.

The style of using designations as attributes is now frequently used and it is of special importance to. the spoken word medium. Thus we generally say, "President Clinton", not "The American President, Mr. Bill Clinton". Several words can be saved by choosing the former style.

But the proper form of writing such names must be noted. It would not be correct to say "Prime Minister, Mr. Narasimha Rao". You have either to say, "Prime Minister Narasimha Rao" or "the Prime Minister, Mr. Narasimha Rao".

Abbreviations must be avoided. When they are used, the full form should be used alongwith the short form when the name occurs for the first time in your bulletin and then the abbreviation can be used. Nothing should be left unexplained, as far as possible. Thus say, "the leader of the Communist Party of India Marxist, CPI(M), Mr..." and if in the same story the name of the party occurs again the CPI(M) can be used.

EXERCISES:

1. Scrutinise reports in the daily press and find out the common errors therein.
2. Make a list of vowels preceded by the indefinite article 'a' and another of consonants which take the article "an".
3. Listen to the bulletins carefully and find out the errors of drafting, particularly the wrong use of prepositions.

Chapter XIV

VOICED DESPATCHES AND NEWSREELS

Many years ago, there was a minor crisis in the newsroom of AIR in Delhi. The scheduled newsreader failed to report for duty and it was rather late in the evening when an external English bulletin for listeners in Africa was due to go on the air. It was hardly possible to contact any other reader and one of the senior editors volunteered to read the bulletin. In fact, he was overjoyed at the prospect.

Only the listeners were not. One of them made his feelings known in a letter from South Africa. "In a country of so many millions could you find only this voice to read a bulletin?" he asked without making any effort to hide his sarcasm.

The meaning of the comment is quite plain. All those who are connected with radio journalism have to be ready to use their voice without notice. They have to wield the tape recorder with as much ease as they use the typewriter or their pen. Also, they have to train the voice, learn enough to make the voiced despatch should like a professionally rendered radio script and learn to do it effortlessly.

A good and powerful voice is a gift of nature but most of us can, by practice and proper training, learn the technique of raising the voice level once we face the microphone, master the way of handling the microphone, learn how to edit the taped material and prepare our despatch for broadcast.

As we noted in the previous chapter, we can acquire proper understanding of and control over the use of the English language. Likewise, we can acquire a degree of proficiency in the technique of voicing our despatches in English, although it is not our mother tongue and, most of us, do not come from homes where English is habitually spoken.

The broadcast journalists need not and should not aspire to replace a professional news reader. There is thus no need to imitate the latter but he can be a kind of role model and much can be learnt from him by way of modulation of the voice, stressing of words and phrases, allowing pauses between words and sentences and, what is equally important, improving your pronounciation.

Since our effort is always to be intelligible and understood by the audience, the pronounciation must be such as would be understood by the largest possible number of listeners. We may stress again that you do not have to imitate the professional newsreader but you have to achieve clarity in speaking as much as you have to ensure clarity in your writing.

Most of us have our provincial accent which is reflected in our spoken English. In India you can always find out, nine times out of ten, whether a man hails from Bengal, South India, Gujarat or Maharashtra, Punjab or North India from his English accent. In voicing despatches for the radio (and TV) you have to ensure that these provincialisms do not influence your despatch.

The largest number of listeners should be able to follow your despatch without any difficulty and without their ear's sensibility being affected. In both cases the attention of the listener would be diverted and he would not keep track of the news bulletin or the newsreel programme in which your voice is being featured.

All that we have said about using the spoken word style and short sentences, familiar words and similar things have to be carefully noted in writing your despatch which you are going to voice. A despatch has to be written out, like a bulletin, for reading it out. The bulletin is read out by a professional news reader, your despatch is read out by you before the microphone, in the studio or wherever you are recording it, or on the telephone, within the city or long distance, for recording by the newsroom or the control room.

So, there are two clear parts of the exercise: *writing of the despatch* and its *voicing*. Both have to be borne in mind. First you have learnt and practised for some time if you have acted as a bulletin editor or a reporter covering the news for the bulletins. But all that you have learnt must be properly put into practice when you sit down to write your despatch for voicing it for a radio bulletin or for the newsreels.

Radio bulletins can become much better if they carry one or two good voiced despatches in each bulletin. A voiced despatch lends more credibility to the story just as a byline story in a newspaper makes the readers come closer to the event (hopefully). The voiced despatch gives the correspondent much scope for bringing in a personal report, where the first person singular can be justifiably used (without overdoing it).

As far as possible, such despatches should be from a correspondent who is reporting from the scene of action. A foreign correspondent, of course, does it often from his headquarters from where he is covering a number of countries but he can also be asked to visit the scene and report from there.

Of course, you can always ask a senior correspondent to

do a voiced despatch in the form of summing up of an event which he may not have witnessed but the details of which he has gathered and properly assessed.

The despatch, in all these cases, has to be written out in a crisp, striking manner, making it interesting and at the same time fair and objective. If you lose your balance and sensationalise your story the newsroom may either use it, trusting in your judgement, or they may reject it altogether. A voiced despatch cannot be edited. It is unlike a fax, telex or typed story which can be rewritten by the newsroom.

A voiced despatch has thus to be a finished product, both in terms of the contents and the voicing of it. There is only a little scope for editing a voiced version, by way of eliminating the unnecessary pauses and unwanted noises. These get into the report if you have recorded your despatch in an open space or you have been careless to cough or grunt while recording it. For the editing to be done, however, there should be time and the personnel to do it. These facilities and the time may not always be available.

Certain facilities have, of course, to be there. Without proper equipment being installed for recording the despatches received on phone and for playing them into the newscast while the bulletin is being read the talk of voiced despatches is just blowing hot air.

Mental attitudes have to change and editors in the newsroom have to get adjusted to one or two despatches in a bulletin. But more than that the hardware aspect has to be taken care of as much as the correspondents have to ready themselves to voice their despatches.

Broadcast journalism is incomplete without the human voice being employed in the bulletins and the other programmes like newsreels, the voice of the news persons, other than that of the professional newsreader.

Naturally a bulletin will still be dominated by the written script handed to the newsreader in the studio and the voiced despatches will playa supplementary but significant role there. The newsreels programme, however, gives the voice a dominant role and the written commentary or narration by the newsreels editor is just there to link up different despatches and introduce the programme.

The newsreels were devised as a reinforcement of the news bulletins, bringing to the listeners the authentic voices of the main players of the news scene plus interpretative reporting by experienced news persons in their voices. To begin with, the newsreels could be scheduled as a separate programme but they must eventually become part and parcel of the news bulletins.

This means that the newsreels cannot be conceived as a weekly or even daily programme. The listener cannot be expected to wait for a scheduled programme in the evening at the end of the day. He would want analysis and actuality reports several times a day soon after he has heard he news relating to a major event.

In other words, there have to be a number of newsreels everyday so that the listener can wait for the programmes at stated intervals. The despatches can be repeated, with a sentence here and there chopped off, as long as the contents are not dated.

If a story has broken around midday and your first newsreels has been broadcast early in the afternoon, the despatch from a foreign correspondent included in the newsreel could still be valid later in the evening. If the despatch has been filed by a correspondent from within the country he should be doing a different one late in the evening and this could replace the first one.

The newsreels programme thus has to be viewed as a real *adjunct to the bulletin,* elaborating the main news, bringing you the voices of the leaders or personalities who have made the news, and sometimes the voices of the ordinary people who may have a point of view of their own.

The programme should not be seen as a collection of despatches from your correspondents in different parts of the country speaking of the progress of the five year plans, the voices of a number of ministers and other VIPs. They also have a place in such programmes, but only when the events with which they are connected are real news stories and only as part of a news programme.

The broadcast journalist has to equip himself by training and practice to *conceive the news as reported through his and through other voices.* He has to realise that he has to file a despatch in the written word, for being read out aloud by the professional newsreader, and another in his voice reporting the event and also bringing to the listener the voices of some of the important personalities connected with it. By arrangement with the newsroom the first (written) despatch can be dispensed with if his voiced despatch is to be used as a story in the bulletin itself.

For the latter to become possible, the reporter must be trained to use his voice and the newsroom and the control room equipped to record the despatch, listen to it if required before broadcast and for the newsreader to plug the voiced despatch without any loss of time.

Assuming that all these facilities exist and are used, the bulletin editor has to take care not to include too many despatches in a single bulletin. A voiced despatch usually takes thirty to fifty per cent more time than the same story would do if read by the news reader. So, having more than two voiced despatches would cut into your limited time and reduce the bulletin wordage considerably.

This aspect must be borne in mind while deciding how many and how much of such despatches should be covered.

The news reader should be provided the typed version of the despatch to enable him to know when it is going to end and he has to come in again. It also helps him to read the despatch like any other story in case there is some technical failure and the voiced despatch tape cannot be played. The typed version must be part of the bulletin record to enable you to know what has been said before, when you or the succeeding editors do the next bulletin.

The important thing to note is that the journalist in the electronic media must be ready to use the tape recorder and his voice as much as he uses the typewriter. Not only that; his thinking must be permeated by the nature of the medium. The writing part of the bulletin is extremely vital which is why we have paid so much attention to it. It is also linked to the voicing of despatches because the voicing comes only after a despatch is written.

There can be occasions when there is no script. You may be too hard pressed for time to get a despatch ready in typed form. The bulletin may be going on the air in a little while and the lines may be all tuned up for you to speak to the recording people in your newsroom. In such circumstances you have to be ready to do a spontaneous despatch without the aid of a written script. With practice you can acquire the ability to speak extempore.

In any case, when you interview people you do not have the facility of a script. You can, of course, think of the questions you are going to raise and, if the time permits, even draft them on paper, although you cannot read them while interviewing the personality concerned. A certain amount of ad-libbing is an essential part of the broadcast journalist's makeup, training and routine.

That should not, however, lead you to depend on your ability to improvise and forget the essential duty to prepare a script before the voicing part starts.

The broadcasting organisations have to realise that the challenge from the immensely more popular medium of TV can be partly met if the bulletin is made more interesting by having one or two voiced despatches, along with the news reader's voice taking care of the bulk or large part of it. Dull and drab bulletins can be enlivened in this manner.

Secondly they have to understand that the bulletins have to have the newsreel component more than once a day to supplement the bulletin and make your news programmes much more interesting and attractive.

EXERCISES:

1. Write on the importance of voiced despatches and newsreels.
2. A broadcast journalist is not complete until he is equipped to use his voice in reporting and editing news, comment.
3. Form a team of your co-students and prepare a newsreel on a major national event. Compare it with the one broadcast by the radio.

Chapter XV

INTERACTION WITH OTHERS

The bulletin editor cannot function in a state of splendid isolation. He is naturally not in direct touch with the various developments, not even those happenings in the national capital where he may be working. But he has to be in touch with the Pool, where it exists, the reporters' room which may be turning out some new story or the new version of a developing item. If there is no Pool to assist him he has to watch the news agency teleprinters.

Above all, he has to interact with the newsreader who is going to read his bulletin, if his bulletin is going to be read in English. In some cases, like Hindi in AIR, the bulletin is prepared in the language of broadcast. So what we say here about interaction with the news reader applies to such bulletins and their editors also.

There is need also for interaction between the editor of the bulletin and the translating unit or units if the script prepared by the editor is meant for translation and then broadcast in that language or languages.

Years ago, we in the AIR newsroom were puzzled by repeated complaints that our external bulletins were still referring to the African nation of Malagasy by its old name - Madagascar. Puzzled because we had given everyone instructions to use only 'Malagasy' - the group of editors who were assigned to the bulletins addressed to listeners in Africa, the stenographers typing out the script at great speed and the newsreaders who took turns reading the bulletins. And yet the complaints!

Suddenly one day, an alert newsreader walked into my office (I was then Chief News Editor, in charge of the newsroom). He did not say "eureka" but I could read it on his face as he pointed out that the complaints were justified. V.M. Chakrapani (that was his name) draw our attention to the opening announcement of the bulletin which, indeed, carried the old name. "THIS IS ALL INDIA RADIO BROADCASTING TO LISTENERS IN EAST AND SOUTH AFRICA, MADAGASCAR, ..."

The trouble arose because the opening announcement of the bulletin was being copied from bulletin to bulletin in a mechanical manner. The editor would handover that page only when he was ready to dictate the headlines and would not have the time to read through the announcement, although he is supposed to read it. He just checked the headlines after they were typed.

The editor ought to have corrected the mistake in the opening announcement, any of the news readers ought to have noticed the mistake, one of the stenographers could have detected it. The last named should not have typed out the announcement mechanically in the face of the written instructions. It was left to Chakrapani, however, to notice the error and his alertness saved AIR further embarrassment which was occurring in spite of the instructions repeatedly brought to the notice of the three different categories of the staff involved in the exercise.

The incident has been referred to here only to underline the role that a news reader can play. He is there not merely to read the bulletin which is, of course, his main job. He is an integral part of the news process. He is the one who delivers the final product to the listener. He is, of course, selected for the job of reading for his ability to read the script intelligently, clearly and correctly, his voice quality and his ability to stress the words and phrases properly, and to have the knowledge and ability to use the right accent and pronounciation. But, additionally he is also a part of the process of making and delivering the bulletin.

Interaction with him is thus of much consequence to the success of your bulletin. He must hand over the pages of the script to read well in advance of the broadcast time. The editor and he must now and then exchange a word or two about the developments taking place which may influence the final structure of the bulletin. If he is kept informed, broadly without getting into the details, he would be able to bring a more informed mind to bear on his reading.

It is fashionable for some news persons to treat the newsreader as a mere ornamentation and some of the readers also do not take themselves seriously, being content with stressing and assuming an air of profundity in the matter of accent and pronounciation. The importance of correct rendering of names and persons and places cannot be overemphasised. A system of guiding the news readers about the correct rendering of names, whether from your own country or abroad, must be part of the news operations.

Some news readers take excessive care about foreign names but do not give enough attention to the names within the country. In India, for example, names written in English do not give one an idea of the correct pronounciation of those names. In AIR, there is a system of rendering these names, and even the foreign names, in the Devnagari script which is scientific. Whatever the system, the important point is that it must be followed.

The pronounciation of foreign names must be ascertained from the foreign language units in your own organisation or from other knowledgeable people, including the embassies of those countries.

The interaction with the news readers has to be continuous. No drill can be laid down and naturally the news reader would come to know of the developments being reported because he rehearses the pages on which the stories are typed.

But that does not mean that the two - the editor and the newsreader - function in two different compartments. In AIR, the General Newsroom (GNR) is so designed that while the editor carries on his work in his allotted area of operation and the news reader rehearses the pages in his, there is scope for them to know what is going on in the GNR and what stories are going to develop. They can know, if they keep their eyes and ears open, what is cooking. The Pool is busy with its work, the other bulletin desks are engaged in their work but if they so desire they would surely know what is happening where in that big, long room (a big hall) with a variety of desks and bulletin compilation work in progress.

The interaction between the bulletin editor and his newsreader is of great importance. The newsreader is the one who is going to read the script aloud and he can tell the editor what the effect of a particular drafted sentence would be like. If your bulletin has said, "the Congress (I) party won two seats in the election and the Janata Dal and the BJP won one each", the newsreader should be the person to draw your attention to the fault. Not the facts, which is your area of responsibility but the error of saying "won one each". You would notice that "won" and "one" have almost identical pronounciation and unless the script is changed to say, for example, "secured one seat each", there is bound to be some confusion in the mind of the listener.

So, the newsreader's suggestions and comments should be heard with respect and, where possible, they should be accepted with grace and gratefulness.

Such suggestions would naturally pertain to the writing

part of the bulletin, more particularly to the proper use of the definite and indefinite articles, prepositions and the choice of words in some places. If any factual error comes to the notice of the news reader while he is rehearsing the bulletin he should also bring this to the editor's notice.

All changes have, however, to be made with the consent and knowledge of the editor who is ultimately responsible for what is broadcast. Bad blood between the editor and the newsreader can be avoided and harmony and cooperation can be strengthened if the editor is consulted before effecting any change in the script of the bulletin.

Both have thus to work in tandem. This cooperation is specially essential inside the studio where the bulletin is to be read out by the newsreader for broadcast. The news reader has to report well in advance of the broadcast time, rehearse the pages and go to the studio about five minutes before the broadcast time. This time of five minutes should be utilised by him to draw a deep breath and get himself mentally prepared for the broadcast so that he puts himself in the right frame of mind for the reading.

By the time the news reader has installed himself in the studio chair the first few pages of the bulletin script, along with the headlines page, must be in his hands. The first few pages could constitute the entire first bunch of the bulletin or a major part of it. The remaining pages must follow quickly thereafter and should be placed in neat bunches in front of the news reader.

The reader must be ready for last minute changes in the bulletin pages, that is, in different stories. Mainly such changes will be confined to the last few pages to enable the editor to see that the sports stories are read, any headline items placed towards the end of the bulletin, including sports headlines, are read and important stories received after the bulletin began are also read.

The editor must, however, refrain from making too many changes In fact, he must ensure that only the most unavoidable changes are made and the news reader's concentration is not disturbed. The latter can give of his best if he is not asked now and again to drop something and read something he has not rehearsed, or read something in a different order. The news reader is not a machine.

But the reader has to be ever ready to read a few lines without rehearsing to accommodate stories received too late for rehearsal or received after the broadcast is on the air. He must not act fussy and not resent the slightest rearrangement of the order of items or feel disturbed by the presence of another editor or even the editor of the bulletin himself.

This again underlines the need for continuous interaction between the editor and the news reader. The latter's speed of reading must also be taken into account. Although the news readers are expected to read at a uniform speed some variation in the pace takes place between any two newsreaders. This means the editor has to keep some extra stories in hand, if the reader has a reputation for fast reading and be prepared to crowd out one or two stories if the news reader is known to go slow.

The editor has to interact with the translating unit or units as much as he interacts with the newsreader, if the bulletin has to be translated and then broadcast instead of being broadcast in English. This interaction is all the more essential because the translating units are generally located at a distance from the bulletin editor. While he is operating from the newsroom the translating units are located in some other part of the building. In the case of the units of the foreign languages they are generally at a considerable distance from the newsroom.

This physical barrier has to be broken. The translating units have to feel they are equally part of the news process, as much as the editor of the bulletin given to them for translation. They are actually news units. It is only a matter of convenience that the script is prepared first in English and sometimes a single editor does a common script for several units. But the news is ultimately put out by them and the listener knows only the relevant newsreader as the one who brings the news to him.

Some of these news readers have become household names in their respective linguistic regions. For many of the listeners the news organisation is synonymous with the news reader. Audiences identify themselves with the newsreaders. The same for the TV news presentors too. As long as the system of the news being presented, not by the editor who has compiled the bulletin but by a professional reader, continues to be in force the news reader whether in English or one of the languages in which the script is translated will continue to be an important part of the bulletin process.

The editor has to bear the convenience of the translating units in mind and also be aware of the problems they would face if they have to throwaway well edited and translated material. The pages of the bulletin must be made available to them at stated intervals. The headlines page, with the order of items indicated thereon, must be in the hands of the units a half hour before the time of broadcast of the first of the bunched builetins. Whenever necessary the units should be given a different set of headlines.

Changes in the items must be kept to the minimum so that the units do not have to discard transalted stories and undertake additional work. The units have, however, to be ready to do it when the needs of the bulletin so dictate and the changes become absolutely unavoidable. The editor must follow the guidelines given in an earlier chapter on compilation so that the 'irreplaceable' items are first edited and sent away for translation. Only such stories as you regard as absolutely imperative and most unlikely to change should be first covered.

The translating units have also to be ready to interact and get involved in the news process. Some of them may be too happy to be left alone to plough their lonely furrow. This is hardly desirable in a news organisation. The editor should keep them informed of the actual and expected news developments. There should be more communication between the units and the bulletin editor who should visit the units once in the shift and the units should also make it a habit to visit the editor.

It is when the interaction breaks down or is just not there that the kind of embarrassing situation we saw earlier on - some AIR bulletins going on the air without the story of the ouster of the former Soviet President - can be avoided.

Translation is actually a creative activity. The translator creates a story in his language following the facts and the presentation in the original script. (These must be strictly adhered to.) The translator gives his listeners the feeling that he is bringing the news to him in the original. He must not let them feel that the stories were first written in a foreign language and then rendered in the language of broadcast.

There is thus no need for the editor to look down upon the translators. They actually are performing a difficult task, that of rendering at great speed news from a foreign language in their own. They on their part must not feel that the editor of the bulletin is a distant person. On both sides there must be an effort to bridge the communication gap. The pages of the bulletin must not be the only point of contact between the two sides.

EXERCISES:

1. Why is interaction important between the editor and the news reader?
2. Write on the importance of the news reader as an essential part of the news process.
3. What measures would you suggest for breaking down the barriers between the editor and the translating units?

Chapter XVI

CORRECTING MISTAKES IN BROADCASTS

In spite of your best efforts mistakes can occur in the bulletin. As we have emphasised, facts have to be checked, the sources of news have to be really dependable before you put your trust in them and, in special cases, you may even wait for confirmation of a story from a second source before you broadcast it.

Your drafting may be flawless and you maya check the script of the bulletin and the headlines carefully before you send the bulletin pages into the studio for the news reader to read them. The latter may have rehearsed the bulletin dutifully and may be his usual careful self while reading it out in the studio. Notwithstanding all these careful steps mistakes can occur.

The source you may have depended upon may not be truthful or may not have checked his facts. An allegation made by one party or individual may be denied by the affected party. The other side of the picture may be brought out by the party which is concerned with the story. You might slip up in writing the story. Finally, the news reader himself or herself may go wrong and make a mistake.

In all such cases, it is not only desirable but necessary for you to carry a correction in your bulletin. If it is still on the air while a mistake is detected the correction should be rushed to the studio and read out as a fresh story. It should be read out with the preface: "Here is a correction."

The newsreader's mistakes should be corrected by him if he detects them or the editor standing by his side there does so. The correction should be preceded by the worlds: "I beg your pardon. I shall read that again." If he has proceeded to other stories and the mistake is detected at correction. "Here is a correction in the news item broadcast earlier in this bulletin about... "

Even if the mistake has been left in the script by the editor and the news reader detects it only while reading the bulletin, he must say;" I beg your pardon. I shall read that again."

It is good manners to ask for pardon if a mistake has occurred. It is bad manners to read on even after detecting the mistake or just say; "I shall read that again. "Why again, if you have not made a mistake? If a mistake has been committed, asking for pardon is only a matter of courtesy to the listeners.

The listener is not concerned with who made the mistake in the first place, the editor or the newsreader. As we have said again and again, the listener knows the news broadcast from what the newsreader tells him. the news reader gets a lot of credit from the listeners for the should, therefore, not feel hesitant to acknowledge the mistake while he is on the air whoever the author of the mistake may be.

As to the news items which are behind by a party affected by it, it is obligatory for you to carry the correction in the next available bulletin of that series.

Of course, the denial must come from a proper source. Any statement issued by a third party is not a denial. It is only another expression of views and you have to evaluate it as a news story on its merits.

The radio of all the media of news operates at great speed. It is truly an instant medium. Mistakes can, therefore, occur in broadcasting news and we have seen how they can happen at any of the various points through which a news item passes before it actually goes on the air. So long as a mistake is not made in a mala fide manner no motives can be ascribed to you, provided you take care to put out a contradiction once the mistake is detected.

Let us suppose that the leader of a certain political party has been assaulted while engaged in some public activity. The first version, as reported by your sources and as alleged by him, may be that he was assaulted by the activists of another party. Once you broadcast a news item to that effect, the other party will come out with its own version.

That version has also to be broadcast in the next bulletin of that series. You can carry it as an independent item but a reference to the earlier story may be necessary. If you ignore the version of the other side, you lay yourself open to the charge of one-sided and partisan presentation of news. This must be avoided.

Sometimes the identity of a known public figure is mixed up in the report and there have been cases where the news of the death of that person has been carried wrongly. The mistake may have been committed by the source. Even so, you have to put out the correction because you owe it to your listeners to give them the facts. You have taken the responsibility of carrying the original story.

The need for being careful and for checking facts before broadcasting the news thus becomes patently clear. But somebody somewhere slips up and you become the vehicle of incorrect news, some of which may cause even a consternation.

In 1979, the then Prime Minister of India, Mr Morarji Desai, announced in the Lok Sabha (lower house of Parliament) that a highly respected public figure,

Jayaprakash Narayan, was dead. J.P., as he was lovingly called, was lying critically ill in a leading hospital in Bombay and in the circumstances, death could have taken place any time.

But the announcement was not true. The leader was very much alive. Since the news came, virtually from the horse's mouth, AIR carried the news and the complexion of its other programmes was also changed in deference to a great leader's memory. The mistake was detected by AIR's own correspondent at the hospital who had seen JP alive just then and after checking once again he got in touch with the newsroom in Delhi. By that time the source which had misled the Prime Minister had also discovered his mistake.

About the reporting of the death of such outstanding figures there are standing instructions. But since JP was not a government VVIP the rules were perhaps not followed. In any case, there cannot be a better source than the Prime Minister speaking in Parliament. But the ordinary precaution of getting confirmation of the death of a prominent person, any other person for that matter, from a hospital or a doctor before reporting it has to be remembered.

Except in such extraordinary cases, the editor has to go ahead and carry the news if he is satisfied about the factuality and if you are ready to broadcast a contradiction when and if the story is denied. You cannot spend a great deal of time confirming a story, from "both ends", so to speak.

Once in AIR we received a story from the only national agency in operation then, the *Samachar,* that some persons travelling with the Congress leader, Mrs Gandhi, then out of power, had been caught and punished for ticketless travel. Mrs Gandhi was on her way to Aligarh from Delhi and the story had come from *Samachar's* Aligarh correspondent.

The story made news (It was a box item in several newspapers the next day.) There was no way of confirming it and we felt (I was then Director of AIR's News Services Division) we could not miss the story. It was carried and promptly denied by the party's spokesman. We carried the denial also, in all the bulletins which had carried the earlier story. But this did not satisfy the party which asked why it was broadcast at all. Surprisingly, even the people in power felt that way. They felt, in a kind of inverted sense of media responsibility, that the story was deliberately done to put them in the wrong in the eyes of the opposite on and the people.

Years later, I happened to meet the correspondent who had filed the story. He confirmed that he had done it after getting the news from a journalist, belonging to a newspaper owned by the Indira Gandhi family. That person had travelled with the party from Delhi and was a witness to the incident but was in no position to use a story adverse to the Congress (I) party himself. The only flaw in the *Samachar* correspondent's story was that he had not confirmed the story from the railway authorities.

The incident has been recalled here to show the kind of problems faced in the selection and presentation of news. Everything that was required to be done was done, the source was a reliable one, the only national news agency at that time, and when the story was denied by the party the denial was carried. The entire approach was above board and there was nothing *mala fide.*

If the story had a prominent leader of the party at the centre we could have gone to some further extent to confirm it from him or the party spokesman or the railway authorities. Here, only some unnamed followers were involved. But in doing our professional duty we had been suspected by the powers that be of doing it deliberately to create problems for them.

Yet one's professional duty must be done no matter what the consequences.

When we talk of corrections or inserting a late message in the bulletin while it is on the air, we are actually dealing with the deliberate action of interrupting the bulletin to catch the listener's attention. We deem the news item of special significance. We see in it news of special value and urgency which we cannot afford to make the listener wait for until the next hourly bulletin or the next bulletin in the series.

In other words the story also must stand up to that significance. There are again two kinds of stories which have to be broadcast by interrupting a bulletin apart from the correction. One is a late message and the other is a flash. To speak first of a flash message, this appendage must be sparingly used. The occasions when you may insert a flash in a running bulletin are a major national tragedy, a resignation which could topple a government in your own country or in a neighbouring country of much consequence to your nation, a military coup in your own nation or the neighbouring country, the death of a highly important political figure or similar stories.

The flash should be introduced: "Here is a flash. "Then you may add: "Further details are awaited. To continue with the bulletin." In other words, the flash should be demarcated from the rest of the bulletin.

The flash story must also be the first headline to be repeated and must be taken as the lead of any succeeding bulletin. (In AIR, Hindi and English bulletins follow one another in many cases.)

This advice also applies to the second category of stories which are used in the bulletin by interrupting it. These stories are of considerably less significance than a flash item and should be introduced as: "Here is a message received after the bulletin began." The story deserving of this prominent treatment must be really important and urgent. It may be, for example, the actual happening of an expected development to which you may have made a reference in your bulletin already. If you had said Mr so-and-so is expected to resign and there are unconfirmed reports of his resignation and before your bulletin ends confirmation of the resignation is received you can insert a late message.

There can be other occasions too. The story, in other words, must be important enough but not an earth-shaking development that may require you to broadcast it straight-away as a "flash". The late message should usually be taken as the first item in the repeated headlines.

It goes without saying that the Pool or whoever is in charge of the newsroom must do a considerable amount of followup on the flash story or the message just received so that the story receives adequate notice in subsequent bulletins. The followup action may also have to be taken by the reporting staff.

A word more about the corrections to be broadcast. There have been cases when the corrections were not properly drafted and the purpose of making amends for a mistake was defeated. For example, if you are correcting your earlier story about the death of a prominent person you must not say: "We regret that our earlier story of the death of so-and-so is not true." This would imply that you are sorry that that person is not dead which is not what you want to convey. You should say something like this: "In our bulletin broadcast at 9 p.m. last night we had reported the death of Mr so-and-so. This report, received from ... was wrong. We regret our error."

EXERCISES:

1. Why is if necessary to broadcast corrections and in what circumstances should you do it?
2. How would you distinguish between a flash and a late message? Give examples.
3. What care would you exercise in broadcasting denials?

Chapter XVII

PRIMACY OF SPORTS NEWS

More and more people are turning to sports watching, either live in the playing grounds, stadia and sports arenas, or on the TV which brings a large number of sports events to you as they happen. The Radio has been doing it for many many years. The newspapers are devoting much space to sports coverage. Events at home naturally are given a lot of attention but international sports stories are also being featured.

This is one area of human activity where a large number of listeners are more knowledgeable than the bulletin editor. This point has to be well understood by the broadcast journalists. You can ignore sports at the peril of losing your audience if you are facing competition and losing credibility if you are not.

When a man comes home from work in the early evening hours, he expects you to tell him of the results of major events that he would know are due to be played that day or special stories about sports and sportsmen or sportswomen. *Your failure to do so would hardly be forgiven.* You have to make a special effort to bring the latest results and some details of major events through your bulletin.

As we have observed, many of the editors are not fond of sports stories. It is perhaps due to lack of interest and inability to understand the finer points of the games. Or it may be due to the faulty approach that a journalist doing sports stories is an inferior type.

This approach has to be corrected. All the more because no bulletin is complete without its complement of sports stories and without the results of events that have taken place by the time you go on the air. Sports bulletins have their place and live relays have theirs. The regular news bulletins, whether the hourly sports news or the scheduled ten minute ones, have their special place as vehicles of news and these must carry all the relevant sports stories.

The editors have to acquire a minimum of grounding in understanding and drafting the sports stories. You do not have to be specialists in sports any more than you have to be a crime investigator to report crime stories or an expert in political science to cover Parliament, assembly or any political party activities. A good journalist has to be a jack of all trades and sports.

Because sports help you to retain your liveliness, your national pride is involved or because sports provide a point of escape from the strains and stresses you are subject to, the number of sports lovers, as opposed to those who can play or have played some major game or the other, is legion. This point has to be grasped clearly by the editors so that sports stories get their due in your bulletins.

A modicum of interest and understanding will help you to evaluate the stories and the results, what to play. up and what to play in a low key, what controversies to highlight and which ones to ignore.

This is necessary because so many results would be available and you may be baffled having to decide what to carry and what to leave out. The rigid principle of selection and brevity of presentation has to be applied to sports stories as to any other story.

The average listener would want you to give the results of major events and some interesting details which help him to understand why a certain thing happened. It is not enough, for example, to say "at this stage there was a sudden collapse in the South African batting". You must also say who brought about that collapse, namely the bowlers of the Indian side and they must be named.

If an expected event has failed to come off even that non-occurrence has to be reported. If, for example, a test match could not be played because of rain or bad light that is also news. The number of sports knowing people is much large, as we have pointed out.

Even otherwise, the failure of an expected event to happen is itself news, like the failure of a political party's convention to be held because the leadership could not agree on the resolutions to be moved or some other reason. The police refusing permission. to hold the convention would be news by itself.

Sports stories should also be considered for headlining usually the fourth headline in a ten minute bulletin. If by the time it is repeated the picture has changed - say, one of the two teams have scored a goal - that information must be covered in the repeated headline. Remember you are enlivening your bulletin by its sports component and by headlining a story you are keeping the listener waiting until the detailed story is reached in the bulletin. You have to appreciate that many listeners turn to your bulletin just to get the latest sports news.

The writing of sports stories is somewhat different from the writing of the other, general stories. Our approach in doing the latter is to be strictly factual and eschew all frills and adjectives. Sports stories are, on the contrary, given special treatment, adjectives like a splendid goal, a glorious century, a miraculous save (by the goalkeeper in hockey or football), dogged defence, a spectacular six are some of the expressions usually associated with sports news items.

The same applies to the writing of the sports headlines too. The newsreader has also to read the sports stories with some gusto and feeling which must be avoided in the reading of other stories.

Sports stories are by convention placed towards the end of the bulletin and the headline also comes at the end of the four or five headlines. There can, however, be occasions when an outstanding sports story can provide you with a lead and then the first headline will also come out of that story.

But such events can be very rare. Your national team winning the world cup of hockey, football or cricket or a sportsman of your country winning a world title, as in boxing, badminton or any other major game, your national team winning an Olympic gold medal or if they are habituated to win, their emerging first in the medals tally are among events when the sports stories can be placed ahead of the other stories or even be the lead of the bulletin.

Towards the end of the bulletin the editor in the studio has to guide the newsreader to ensure that the sports stories, in general and the headline item in particular, are not crowded out. Some editors place the sports story or stories ahead, much too ahead, of other stories so that automatically the sports story would be covered.

This is not a healthy practice, not to be followed from day to day. Generally the sports stories must be followed by the weather reports and forecast and then the end of the bulletin could be announced after repeating the headlines. You may keep an item or two small items after the sports story, if there is no weather report now and then but to make a habit of broadcasting the sports story, say, in the seventh or eighth minute of a ten minute bulletin is not to be commended.

The fairness and balance in covering news in general

must also be reflected in sports stories. Naturally, the national teams and players would get all the attention that you can devote in your stories, but the performance of the opposite sides must also find mention. Partisanship in sports is widely prevalent but good reporting requires that both sides should be presented in a balanced manner.

Another point to be noted by editors doing sports stories is that sports must be covered in a continuous fashion. There is a tendency to give the sports stories a go-by when there is pressure of political stories in the bulletin. This attitude of accommodating sports only when you can do so results in some disjointed coverage of events which may not be deserving a place in a major bulletin and the sudden disappearance of a major sports story.

All this calls for a little more interest in sports among the editors so that the sports stories are not ignored or crowded out. If you make it a point that all interesting sports events would find a place in your bulletin you will be able to make the necessary adjustments in other stories and find time for the sports stories to be covered.

Covering items which need not be covered and leaving out the major ones when you are hard pressed for time leaves a bad taste in the mouth of the listener. As we have noted, the listeners are keenly interested in sports and are also quite knowledgeable about the various competitions and tournaments. They can easily make out if you are doing your sports stories in a knowledgeable manner or mechanically.

If we have laboured here the point about the primacy of sports in news the reason is quite clear. Experience has shown that many editors are neither aware of the importance nor sufficiently interested in the major games to be able to handle stories with any degree of satisfactory performance.

For example, the Indian TV network would often say the match is in an interesting stage when it has actually ended and the interested viewer has learnt about it from the radio's running commentary relaying a ball-by-ball description. That the TV editors have not cared to find out the latest state of the game speaks both of their disinterest and the poor organisational arrangement to get the latest news.

Such apathy and non-chalant attitude must end and give place to a lively interest and awareness so that both the knowledgeable and the lay listeners are served.

EXERCISES:

1. Write of the primacy of sports news and why the broadcast journalists should be aware of it.
2. When can a sports story take precedence over other news items of a general nature?
3. What should an editor do to accommodate all the relevant sports stories in his bulletin even if the pressure of other stories is heavy?

Chapter XVIII

INSTANT NATURE OF RADIO

In many countries the radio is on the air round the clock. In India listeners can get AIR on the FM channel late at night and early in the morning. Programmes at that hour carry the hourly bulletins and the one who goes to bed late at night or rises unusually early can get to hear the news. Those who are driving or travelling by a long distance bus or train can also listen in.

There are occasions when a large body of listeners are awake to hear some news to which they attach great importance, like results of a national election. The hourly bulletins come into their own at that time and have a much larger audience than usual. There can be similar other events which the audience would follow right through the night while some listeners would switch on their sets early in the morning if they had gone to bed during the night. In a national crisis of political nature the interest is heightened and the radio bulletins are the only means to satisfy it.

That is so because the newspapers can appear only once in a day and it is not often that they come out with a special supplement. Also because even the TV is not on the air during those unearthly hours. If there is a channel showing some old movie or a special entertainment programme the programmers are hot equipped to switch over to news at short notice.

The radio is thus unique in that it is always on the air and if a radio programme is on the air you can be sure that there will be a bulletin at stated intervals, generally an hourly news broadcast. In other words, the radio is well prepared to go into action as a medium of news because, unlike the other media, it is always there. When everybody else is fast asleep the radio's newsroom is awake, like the Yogi of the *Bhagwadgita* who "is awake when it is night for all the beings." (Chapter 11-69).

The newsroom can well boast: "We never close." People there are working either to put out a bulletin on the hour or keep stories ready for the others who come early in the morning to prepare their bulletins.

It is not the readiness to handle stories and broadcast bulletins at all odd hours, without much notice, that alone distinguishes the radio as an instant medium from the other media of news. There is a certain degree of simplicity of operation and smoothness and speed in handling news which marks the radio's newscasts. This ensures that the radio can go on the air with the latest news at any given time of the day or night.

The newspapers close down their operations at 2 a.m. or so each morning when the last city edition is being got ready for printing. They come alive, that is their editorial offices, only around nine or ten next day. As we saw in an earlier chapter, the Indian newspapers had gone to bed after announcing that the "Arabian desert was tense but quiet" on January 17, 1991 and when the papers were being read by the readers the war had begun in a fierce and bloody manner.

Many of the papers came out with supplements by noon or early in the afternoon but by then the radio had broadcast several bulletins giving a lot of information about the Gulf war. Since then the only supplement one can remember to have seen was when Rajiv Gandhi was assassinated near Madras in May that year.

With all their sophistication and the development of the infrastructure of printing the newspapers cannot function as instant medium of news. The TV also needs a longer time spread to go into action. It is only the radio which can go on the air almost without notice. Once the infrastructure of transmission is in position and the news people are at their job - they are always there as we have seen - the radio is ready to give you the latest news developments.

No wonder, leaders of a military coup seize the radio station in the national capital the first thing after seizing power and use it to announce that they have arrived.

All this imposes on the editors a heavy responsibility. It is upto them to justify the honour of being the instant medium by their split second response to developments and going on the air to bring to the listener the latest without any loss of time. Alertness, quick reflexes and display of editorial ability to make, up a bulletin and broadcast it are called for if the radio has to live up its reputation of an instant medium.

It is not the editor in the newsroom alone who has to play that role. The radio's reporter, in the field and at the headquarters, has also to be fully involved. So also the others who are connected with the news operations, including the newsreaders.

Several years ago, the then Prime Minister of India, Mr Morarji Desai, was on tour in the north-east of the country when the Indian Air Force plane by which he was travelling crashlanded. It was around ten in the evening when the news filtered down to the knowledgeable in the capital. Our 9 p.m. bulletin (I was then Director of News Services) had reported his departure for the north-east region.

A highly placed person contacted me to know if we had received any news about the safe landing of the Prime Minister. I was then just home and promised to let him know after checking with the newsroom. I found the night editor-in-charge had no information from any source and, indeed, he was not aware that the plane had crashlanded.

I knew that an alert reporter had accompanied the Prime Minister and told the newsroom chief to watch 'out for his despatch. The reporter K. Govindan Kutty, now with the *Indian Express,* Delhi, was known for his enterprise and keenness but I advised the editor-in-charge to do everything possible to get the story from any other - sources the Defence ministry sources, news agency, our own news units in Assam - while Kutty's report was awaited.

The reporter fully justified our hopes. He had walked three or four kilometres to get to the nearest telephone to tell us that though the plane had crashlanded the Prime Minister was unhurt. We could tell the listeners the story of his escape in our 11 p.m. hourly bulletin and allay the anxiety and fulfil the expectations of the knowledgeable while keeping the lay listener informed.

But for the reporter's initiative we could not have got the story for many hours, not even the next morning. There was a national news agency correspondent on the same plane and, along with Kutty, he too walked the same distance to get hold of the trunk phone. But his desk in Calcutta could not hear him properly or something went wrong and his story was not received before it was too late. On the other hand, the AIR newsroom was alerted in advance and was all keyed up to receive Kutty's story and put it out in the nearest bulletin which was at hand.

Even in the absence of competition from a rival radio station or network the role of the instant medium could be performed if there is all-round awareness of that role and everybody is prepared to play his part. Facts have to be checked and accuracy and reliability have to be ensured but they should not become excuses for delay and for inaction. Sensationalism not to be encouraged, specially in a medium like the radio, but failure to deliver and playing for safety is not only unprofessional but an act of letting down the listener.

In other words, the men who operate the medium have to rise to the occasion and make full use of its potential. Alertness which we generally know as 'nose for news' is an asset and all newsmen have to develop it to be able to perform their primary function of being first with the news.

There have been many instances when AIR's reporters have brought in stories which the agencies covered much later and, in fact, after AIR had put them wise about the events. Once the Bombay correspondent filed a story about the crash of an Air India plane soon after takeoff from there. This was a case of a happening after the newspapers had gone to bed and the agency's guard was also lowered. The radio reporter just came to know of a crash, got busy, collected all the details and called the newsroom in Delhi well in time for the morning bulletins to give the nation the bad news.

Thus much depends on the broadcast journalist's understanding of his role and his zeal and devotion to duty, Technical arrangements have to be kept in readiness for receiving the news pertaining to a major national development but the journalists have to prepare themselves to handle the job.

An event may be expected to take place close to your hourly bulletin or a scheduled major bulletin. It could go one way or it could go the other way. Either way it, is of much consequence. In 1975, the Supreme Court of India was about to deliver its order on the petition filed by Mrs, Indira Gandhi praying for stay of the Allahabad High Court judgment setting aside her election to the Lok Sabha (lower house of Parliament). If the stay was granted she could continue as Prime Minister, not otherwise.

The order was expected to be made after 3 p.m. which meant we could take the story in the 4 p.m. hourly bulletin. We had scheduled a Hindi bulletin in addition to the regular English bulletin. And we succeeded in covering the main points of the order in both, although the judge delivered it close to the broadcast time.

It is a different story that the Hindi version which was true and factual was misunderstood by the powers that be and minister I.K. Gujral lost his job soon after when the Emergency was declared. Both the bulletins had factually covered the story but while the English version, made available by the minister, was on the soft side and emphasized the points favourable to Mrs. Gandhi - like she could continue to be a member of the house - the Hindi version, done by an experienced and careful reporter, made it plain that her membership would be devoid of the power to vote in the house.

EXERCISES:

1. How is the radio different from the other media of news to make it an instant medium?
2. What are the duties and responsibilities of the broadcast journalist for making a success of the instant medium?
3. The medium is as good as the men who operate it. Comment.

Chapter XIX

HOW TV NEWS DIFFERS

Our concern in this book has been with radio news and writing for the radio. But essentially both radio and TV are spoken word media and to that extent the guidelines we have framed for broadcast journalism would apply to the TV medium too. The spoken word is the common thread running through both media.

You have to say both in a radio bulletin and TV newscast: "The Japanese Prime Minister is arriving in Delhi *tomorrow*" not on January 15, presuming that you are telecasting the news on January 14. This elementary illustration should be enough to show that both radio and TV are different from the printed medium of the newspapers because both are spoken word media.

The difference between the two media is that the TV news presenter is right there in front of you while the radio newsreader has only to be heard. But because he or she is there and is *speaking* to you the rules of the spoken word medium apply to TV as well as to the radio bulletins.

Of course, the TV medium is a visual medium and the bulletin can be made really interesting by adding film, with or without sound, stills, captions; drawings and charts to the spoken word. Not only adding to the *"dry"* stories, as stories without visuals are known to the TV editors, but presenting the news in the visual idiom, so to say.

The visuals are to be taken in by the eye, unlike the spoken word which is absorbed by the ear. Even the eye is not strained much, as in reading a book or a newspaper, because the visuals are generally in pictures. Even among pictures, the moving one is more acceptable because that is more attractive and causes the least strain to the eye.

The picture also has more impact. (Recall the Chinese saying: "A picture is worth ten thousand words.") Thus TV news has a distinct advantage over the radio counterpart. But it is basically spoken word news and often when the news breaks close to a telecast the story has to be taken dry, just as in the radio , In TV organisations which are not properly organised to add visuals to their stories and have little film footage from within the country, the spoken word predominates. This is particularly relevant to the Indian TV network, Doordarshan.

Yet another area where both have much similarity is the brevity of their stories. Most TV newscasts are of 20-30 minutes duration and if you take out the visuals the wordage will be found to be almost the same as in radio bulletin of ten to fifteen minutes duration. No matter how much the visual content the TV newscast cannot go on and on.

You can have other current affairs programmes to supplement the news bulletins, but the news bulletins have to be compressed within a timeframe of fifteen to twenty minutes, the half hour newscast being really a ten minute visual show plus the word content. The reason why the time duration has to be relatively short has been explained in detail in the relevant chapter and need not detain in us here.

But the visuals have to be relevant to the audience to be of real interest to them. All news has to have relevance and interest for the audience because of the proximity of the event, the consequence or importance it holds for the viewer and other factors which we have dealt with. News has to be both new and interesting information.

Foreign visuals which dominate the TV newscasts in India cannot have much audience appeal. Simply because they are visuals they do not mean much to an audience which is of high school or even a lower level of education. Even to the more educated audiences which watch the English newscasts the foreign visuals have limited appeal. In recent months, there has been an excessive coverage, by way of visuals, of the trouble in Bosnia, the day-to-day developments in Russia, the frequent appearances of the former American President, George Bush, and British Prime Minister John Major and similar visuals from abroad.

The presence of these visuals becomes all the more glaring and less and less relevant when there are no interesting visuals from within the country. There are a few stock scenes of VVIPs arriving and being received by the President and Prime Minister and the same line of VIPs being introduced to them, the various seminars and conferences in the capital, "inaugurated" by the Prime Minister or lesser lights of the Central government, book releases and releases of commemorative stamps.

If there is a train accident there are no visuals, until after two days when a minister may visit the scene, an air accident story is not accompanied by any visuals. That is also the fate of major fire or other accidents outside Delhi, communal disturbances and natural disasters. After the story has become stale and photographs have been seen by the people in the newspapers, the TV may bring you a few visuals, specially if a minister or chief minister is visiting the place.

So, what is of interest to the people is not shown and what is not of interest or of comparatively less interest is shown in abundance. Visuals are supposed to be part of the news stories - how else will they be there? - As such they must be news or matter of interest to the audience at home.

What is said here of the state of affairs in the Indian TV applies to all television news, whatever the country of which the station is part. There have to be visuals of relevance to the audience. Otherwise they would have no more interest and impact than any other visual programme.

Because the telecasts have to have more visual content to make the bulletin interesting much more planning is called for in TV news than even in radio news. So often the death of a noted personality connected with literature or culture is announced but because there is no proper photo library there is not even a still picture to accompany the story.

So, there has to be a good photo library and many pictures in it of non-political personalities. The same applies to stock film or still pictures of places so that you can use them if there is a reference to those places in your bulletins. If you show a street scene from Cuttack, for example, a day before you are telecasting a one-day international cricket match to be played in that city you can enhance viewer interest. Merely seeing the stadium in the live relay would not make the audience understand how different or similar is Cuttack from their own cities a stadium being as good or as bad as any other.

Your stock of film shots or photos must include some known places or places likely to figure in the news. There have been several stories of repairs to the Jagannath temple in Orissa in the TV bulletins but not a single picture of the temple. Since the annual chariot procession of the deities, the 'rathyatra' is covered by Doordarshan there must be some good film material. Only you have to look for it.

Look for it and plan for it so chat you have a large enough stock of stills and shots which you can use at a moment's notice. Not only the pictures and visuals should be there but they should be also be easily accessible and a trained person should be on duty whenever a bulletin is being prepared to assist the editor and the producer.

This is part of the planning we have referred to. Whenever the Prime Minister is going to visit a foreign country a team is sent in advance and some film is shown in advance to show how the host country is getting ready to give "an enthusiastic" welcome to the visiting dignitary and what the country looks like. By the same token, when an Indian cricket team is about to set out on a long tour of a foreign country you should have in your possession a number of stills and shots from that country.

Often the TV is not in a position to show a still picture of an Indian sportsman who has achieved some distinction. This shows both lack of awareness of the visual character of the medium and lack of planning to build up a visuals library be used on such occasions.

The restrictive nature of the news operations, strictly under the government's control, only make a bad situation worse. First there is no appreciation of the real character of the medium. Then there is a terrible dearth, almost a famine, of relevant visuals which can enliven a bulletin and finally there is the unseen control of the authorities which only complicates the situation.

The radio has the same unseen hand holding it back and sometimes pushing it in the wrong direction but it is an older institution, has a well tried system which has stood the test of time, and a trained and experienced band of editors. Also it is the less noticeable of the two media and less in the public eye.

The TV people have to have both long term and short term planning to make their bulletins better and more acceptable to the people even within the constraints of official control. They normally operate on the principle that somebody invites them to cover a particular event. It reminds you of the old newspaper dictum: *we interview people, we are not given an interview.* If the TV decides that they would determine what to cover and not go by what the pressure groups want them to do a sea change would occur in their coverage and the results would be highly satisfactory.

The present approach of going to an event if invited results in a totally indefensible situation like the absence of coverage of an anti-government rally by leading trade unions in Delhi in November 1992. Simply because the organisers of the rally did not "invite" TV to their show the rally was not visually covered. Only a dry story, played down in the main Hindi bulletin and somewhat played up in the English version, was carried on a day when a ruling party rally in Calcutta was extensively covered in film.

The Minister of Information and Broadcasting, who controls both AIR and Doordarshan, expressed surprise in Parliament over the absence of visual coverage of the Delhi rally. This confirmed the fact that there were no order "from above" to the contrary. What was missing was planning. The habit of going to an event for which there are orders or pressure of some kind or the other prevailed.

What is involved is the basic principle that you make every effort to exploit the visual character of your medium. What is involved is the need for building up one's sources of news. Either your own reporters do the job or some other agency does it but in either case you have to plan for it.

The medium imposes an added responsibility on the editors and those who are expected to guide and direct them. All the time you, or your newscast, and the audience are face to face, something which is peculiar to the TV medium. Your shortcomings become immediately apparent, just as your good points are also immediately appreciated and even applauded.

In previous chapters we have emphasised how the radio editors and reporters have to line up proper arrangements so that they can broadcast a story without any loss of time. An event takes place and you bring the news to the people, sometimes almost as it happens. The same approach must guide the TV editors and their bosses.

When I was working as AIR's South-East Asia correspondent I visited West Irian, a group of islands in the far Pacific. The fate of the islands was being decided under what was called an "act of self-choice", that is its status as a United Nations territory, temporarily under the Indonesian government's control, was to be settled by the vote of the assemblies of the tribal people inhabiting the various islands. If they opted for becoming part of Indonesia the temporary status of control from Jakarta would end.

Two assemblies had voted "yes" and the third was to meet in a remote island and if it also said "yes", the issue would be decided in favour of Indonesia which, to use the sports jargon, would then get an unbeatable lead. I was among a group of journalists who had travelled by ship overnight from Jayapura the capital of West Irian to be able to attend the assembly when it voted. After landing one had to walk to the place where the assembly was to meet.

On my way to that place from the temporary pier I had noted the location of the makeshift telegraph office (those were the days of telegrams and cables, no telex, no fax). As soon as the "yes" vote was cast (which was expected) and West Irian virtually became Indonesian territory. I set out for the telegraph office. While I was almost running. I found a cyclist going my way and persuaded him, with some monetary inducement, to take me on his carrier so that I could reach the telegraph office before anybody else could and my cable to AIR Delhi would have precedence over the Reuters correspondent's copy. He was the only international agency man in our group. There was a Tass correspondent too but AIR did not subscribe to that agency those days.

I succeeded in my mission but what I found on the way was revealing. The Reuters correspondent was running like a trained 2,000 metre middle distance runner (the distance was also 2 kilometres). He was trying to beat everyone else but the bicycle helped me to beat him at his game.

In earlier years whenever I visited Jakarta I used to make arrangements with the AFP in .3ingapore (my base) to allow me to file my stories in their daily newscast from the Indonesian capital to the regional bureau in Singapore from where my friends in the AFP would cable my stories to Delhi. That way, with the help of the AFP people the delays in transmission from Jakarta were overcome. The delays were inordinate. If a cable reached Delhi from Singapore in two hours it took almost two day to travel more or less the same distance from Jakarta.

One can write at great length of such cases. The essential point to be noted is that in all such instances of news coverage advance planning is necessary and, of course, a great deal of improvisation, if the target has to be hit and the goal of being first with the news has to be achieved.

A bulletin does not necessarily become a telecast simply because it is presented through the TV medium. To be able to show that it is a better presentation than the radio bulletin about the same time, you have to strain every nerve to enrich its visual content and make it a much better proposition for the viewer to view and listen to than its radio counterpart.

The difference and advantage of a medium with greater impact has to be felt by the audience. The policy constraints are applicable to both radio and TV which are under the same (over) protective umbrella. Even in the radio, as we shall see in the following chapter, the people who work there have to be aware of their responsibility to the listeners. If you are conscious of the man sitting in his drawing room and watching your newscast or listening to your bulletin in the audio medium you should be able to produce better results.

The spoken word aspect has also to be understood better by the TV editors. Now and again the essentials of the spoken word rules are ignored and you find a TV news presenter saying "the winter session of Parliament will begin on the 24th of November" even if it is the middle of November when the bulletin is being telecast.

But the repetition of names and designations of well known personalities is the worst offence against good newswriting. Every time there is a reference to the Prime Minister - and there would be more than one about which there can be no complaint, both his name and designation are used. Such repetitions, sometimes running to more than half a dozen in a fifteen minute newscast jar on the ears.

The facility of correcting one's stories admittedly is not as good in the TV medium as in the radio, sometimes not existent at all. But greater care can be exercised in doing the story for the first time. Knowing as the editors do that there would be four or five items about the Prime Minister the editing has to be done in such a way that the repetitions are cut out in the first instance.

Things have been carried to absurd proportions. If there are three different stories in the same bulletin on the TV about a certain dignitary and they are taken one after the other the person is referred to by both name and designation on all the three occasions. The viewer is left wondering whether you are talking of the same individual. But the doubt is dispelled because, as often happens with Delhi stories, there are visuals showing the dignitary opening his mouth but not able to utter a word.

EXERCISES:

1. How does the TV medium differ from the radio?
2. What is the role of visuals in making the TV bulletin really interesting?
3. Write on the need for advance planning in making the visual content of the TV newscast interesting to the audience.

Chapter XX

FACTUALITY AND CREDIBILITY

The news, whether on the radio, TV or in the newspapers, has to be both factual and credible. The people have to believe you, that you are telling the truth, not hiding something from them, not playing up something which you or your proprietors are interested in and playing down things which they would like you to softpedal.

Factuality and credibility are closely linked together. If you are factual you acquire the reputation of being truthful and, therefore, credible. An occasional lapse from facts may be forgiven by the audience if you have a reputation for being truthful, although that particular bulletin or that story in a bulletin will fail to pass the test of factuality. But if the trust is lost it will be difficult to regain it.

Not reporting an event which the other media, like the newspapers, have covered or may cover the next day causes a decline in your credibility. If you are saying something which is contrary to what the press is saying, generally speaking, it damages your reputation. The press in India has freedom guaranteed by the Constitution. In other countries too, where the electronic media may be under somewhat tight government control, the press has the same degree of freedom or comparatively they are more free.

Thus a variation between your reports and those in the print media is bound to raise doubts in the public mind. Your listeners could be and are generally more numerous than the readers of newspapers. Many of your listeners may not be able to read or buy and read regularly a daily paper. That does not matter insofar as your credibility is concerned. There is a system for information to travel among the people and there is a role which opinion leaders perform and they read the papers.

There is yet another aspect of the question of credibility. The people know or presume to know many things because information also flows by word of mouth. The trend or a general impression travels much faster than the facts or the information about a particular event. People also see what is going on around them. If you go on saying a certain 'bandh' (work stoppage) was not successful but if the people in a particular city were not able to reach their place of work they would from then onwards suspect your truthfulness.

In the ancient Indian book of stories, called the *Panchatantra,* there is a significant verse which reads:

"All things that are not seen or heard,
In science or the sacred word,
All things in interstellar space,
Are known among the populace."

Of course, the people may not have access to all the information all the time. They may also not have the exact information or even may be harbouring a garbled form of the true state of affairs. What, however, matters is that the people form a general impression of important developments, personalities in the news and about the credibility of the sources of information.

It is for you to feed the correct news to the listeners so that they gradually overcome any prejudice that they may have entertained earlier. In the first place if you are believed your effort should be to strengthen that impression. The newspapers are in a competitive market and if they lose credibility they lose business. So they are careful, except those which have an ideological predilection. Others may lean on one side or the other but they carefully watch the circulation trends and make adjustments in their coverage.

Almost all newspapers have favourites and those whom they do not like, among the leading politicians or prominent personalities in culture, sports and other areas of public interest. When we say "newspapers" we mean the proprietors, editors as well as the key figures in the reporting and writing staff. All the same, the press cannot hide anything. Distortions are often corrected before the paper loses its credibility, circulation and business.

On December 25, 1992 the *Times of India,* known for its pro-Congress(I) and pro-Narasimha Rao government attitude, came out with a story about the deliberations and decisions of the Congress (I) Working Committee, the previous day, loudly proclaiming that the committee had fully backed Rao on the Ayodhya issue. But several other newspapers reported that there were different views in the committee and Rao had not succeeded in carrying the CWC (I) with him.

The very next day December 26, the *Times of India* had to carry a story which contradicted its own previous day's story and put the record straight about the dissenting views in the CWC (I).

The absence of competition for the radio (and TV) may induce them, that is, the governments controlling their news coverage, to distort the coverage to suit their requirements or what they presume to be their interest. But this absence of competition is more apparent than real. There are foreign radio stations to which the people may turn if the national network is not believed. There are satellite TV programmes in which, in the midst of plenty of entertainment or irrelevant programmes, something of real news value may also appear.

As we said, the governments sometimes presume what is their real interest, failing to realize that telling the truth is always better than telling a few lies. Telling lies makes you lose your credibility which means the more knowledgeable may not believe you or may get their information from foreign stations or turn to the other media, like the newspapers.

What do you gain? What do the various governments gain, if the credibility of your electronic media is lost? While the more interested among the listeners may turn away from you the less informed may also lose faith in you.

On December 6, 1992, extraordinary events took place in Ayodhya, the temple town in India's Uttar Pradesh state, where there is a fierce controversy over a shrine. The shrine was pulled down by a mob. News messages were being flashed across the globe but the Indian radio and TV were telling their audiences "the Babri mosque (the shrine) has been *extensively damaged*".

The words may have been appropriate at the early stage of the demolition, not in the later stage, and not when the deed had been done. The two media, however, stuck to that formula all through. Even after the Prime Minister had made a broadcast to the nation in which he used the word "demolition", the media persisted with their phrase "extensively damaged".

Let us not go into the fact that the TV did not show. any shots of the destruction although it had plenty in its possession. Presuming that the total misrepresentation of facts was done at the instance of the government which is known to come down with a "heavy hand" now and again, specially on such occasions, what purpose was served by the distortion, the wholesale lying indulged in by the radio and TV?

Everyone knew that day and later that the shrine had been demolished. There is a vast difference between something being "extensively damaged" and being demolished. The famous venue of national and international conferences in Delhi, Vigyan Bhavan, was "extensively damaged" in fire in April 1990. The damage was repaired and the building was ready for use again less than three years later.

Governments hardly ever learn from experience but the media must know the basic principle of credibility and factuality. In 1977 when the ruling Congress party and its leader, the incumbent Prime Minister Mrs. Gandhi were waging a losing campaign in the Lok Sabha (lower house of Parliament) election, we in AIR repeatedly told the government to let us, report the campaign in a fair and balanced manner. When we had a free hand for the first two weeks or so, the audience heard the bulletins with respect and interest.

But as the government got more and more reports from its intelligence and party sources of its declining fortunes it turned the screw on us and asked fur an excessive share of the news time for the ruling party and permitted just a little for the main opposition, the Janata Party, which eventually won the poll.

Naturally we were not believed and this affected the fortunes of the ruling party even more. If things had been presented in a balanced manner the audiences would have stayed with us and some of the valid points made by the Congress and Mrs Gandhi against the Janata Party, mainly its heterogenous character which led to its fall in two and a half years, would perhaps have been believed.

But, as we said, the government does not learn from experience. The people who succeeded them let us enjoy freedom for a few weeks while the euphoria of their success and their idealistic protestations lasted. Then they clamped down, not as crudely as the predecessors, but the same degree of intimidation of the news staff was practised by them and there was the same dislike of truth.

Media autonomy has been talked about and the Janata Dal government was even able to push through legislation in Parliament in 1990 to create a statutory corporation to run AIR and Doordarshan, free of governmental control. How that corporation would function and what measure of autonomy would be transferred to the operational staff remains to be seen. Unfortunately, the government which got the legislation through the two houses of Parliament, fell and was succeeded by a virtually transitional government. The Narasimha Rao government which came to power in June 1991, after the fall of that government, has made a promise of setting up the corporation but has not done it even in the year 1993.

Meanwhile, what obtains is a rigid system of control on the media, mainly their news coverage and their current affairs programmes, as was the case in the previous Congress regimes, more or less.

On October 31, 1984, when Mrs Gandhi was assassinated by two of her security guards, her elder son, who was considered the most likely "successor to her (and eventually took over), Rajiv Gandhi, was out of Delhi. He was trying to rush to the capital to be on hand for the President to ask him to form a new government. While rushing to Delhi he listened to the radio but found that AIR was putting out the same story bulletin after bulletin - that the Prime Minister had been shot by the two security guards, was gravely injured, but was rushed to hospital for treatment.

Obviously, the same story could not be true for several hours. (Actually Mrs Gandhi was dead.) But the AIR newsroom had orders to say no more until Rajiv Gandhi reached Delhi and was sworn in and then the world would be told that Mrs Gandhi was no more. Rajiv turned to some other foreign stations on his transistor to get the truth even while he was changing planes to reach Delhi.

The point here is not that the credibility of the national radio was damaged by restraining it from telling the whole truth, when everyone knew that Mrs Gandhi was dead, but that Rajiv Gandhi as Prime Minister did nothing to restore the radio's (or TV's) credibility; In this case after a little while, when some air of freedom was breathed, the same rigid system of news management prevailed and his personality was projected from day to day. In one TV bulletin there were as many as seventeen a record but the daily TV bulletin was not substantially different. A trusted aide of his, either from the PMO (Prime Minister's office) or from the Information and Broadcasting ministry, where he was planted, would go down to the TV newsroom every afternoon. He would decide, not the news chief, what should be covered and how much of it and what not. The editors merely carried out the instructions.

Of course, being a corporation there is no guarantee of the autonomy of the media. Unless the people selected to head the corporation and run it from day to day are such as to be imbued fully with the spirit of broadcasting and ready to play fair, no matter who is pleased and who is unhappy, media autonomy will be a chimera. The autonomy has to filter down to the operational level. The editor must feel he can do his job without fear or favour and with only the listener or viewer in mind and with his sense of media responsibility as his guide.

Autonomy thus has to be real and not merely a matter

of form, change from tweedledum to tweedledee, from a government ministry to another body taking its orders and its cue from the ministry.

The unfortunate fact is that while the press is free the electronic media are handmaids of the government, either directly so or through the medium of an "autonomous" corporation. In India, the press enjoys the fundamental right to freedom of expression, which is granted to every citizen. This right has been interpreted by the judiciary as covering the right to freedom of the press. Like all rights, this freedom is subject to reasonable restrictions but the radio and TV have no freedom worth talking about.

The press is in the private sector, owned mostly by individuals or families which have been in this business for long. In most of the countries in South and South East Asia, besides India, the press has a great measure of freedom and in some there is statutory protection also. But TV and Radio are treated differently. The press, by and large, plays an adversary role in most of the countries, although on foreign policy issues it sides with the government, playing a "patriotic" role. There are, of course, some exceptions even in this sphere where an appeal is made to the patriotic instinct of the newspaper media by the ruling organisations.

On the contrary, the radio and TV are taken for granted. Being owned by the government directly or through a nominal corporation they cannot see their way to being an adversary to the government, not even equidistant from the government, and the opposition. Sections of the press are, of course, made to toe the government line and some of them do it willingly to subserve the financial interests of their proprietors. But even they must make a demonstration of their "freedom" from time to time and come out with stories and writings critical of the government. An example has been cited above.

But the radio and TV news media cannot do even that. The explanation for the state of affairs lies in the fact that historically the two media have been "national". In plain terms, they have been financed by the government which keeps a tight control over their operations, news and other programme contents.

Public opinion, meaning the opinion of the political parties, hoping to oust the incumbent government and take its place one day or be in alliance with one which is capable of doing it, generally takes the view that the media must be under "parliamentary" control. This suits the government in power because in the name of parliamentary control the government can keep the media under its thumb. Answerability to Parliament can only be through an "administrative" ministry and that means the government once again.

With deeprooted suspicion of the private operators of the media and the experience of the press barons fresh in their minds the politicians are not prepared to trust them with control of the electronic media. The politicians do not see the danger of their logic, namely, that the ruling party will continue to have a big say in running the media and making them "answerable" to Parliament.

The media cannot thus acquire guts to criticise the government. Will any press let its proprietor be criticised? That is as simple as that. That some of the mediamen have had the courage to carry programmes critical of the government is a tribute to their intrepid conduct. That only goes to prove the rule that unless the media are free of government control they cannot function as creative instruments and free and fair coverage of news can remain a distant goal.

They can, however, be fair and truthful and not indulge in the kind of distortions of the truth to which we have referred earlier. The government have to realise that they harm their owl) interests by trying to dictate what the media should do from day to day. Apart from the necessity felt by them to give the media a broad framework within which they have to operate, the ruling parties should ensure that the media are not subjected to pressures where their truthfulness and fairness are impaired.

Credibility is a delicate plant and has to be nurtured with great care and sensitivity. A violent twist in news coverage and the credibility of the media goes out by the front door. What good will the media be if they are not believed by the people and the latter seek their information and enlightenment from foreign stations or the press media at home?

Of course, there has to be some thinking about the right formula of media ownership and the system that has been successfully operated by countries like Japan and Canada should commend itself to those who are concerned about the freedom of the media. Under this system, there is a great deal of competition between a national network, financed by the government or Parliament, and a number of privately owned stations or network of stations.

Without competition, you cannot make the national network really free and fearless nor can you keep the staff on their toes so that they care for the basic principles of broadcast journalism, are first with the news and are objective, fair and effective. Competition keeps the press free of distortions and makes it reflect different point of view.

The private sector has to be trusted to run the electronic media with as much responsibility as it runs the newspapers. Some element of competition is expected to be provided by the private programmers who will be allotted time on the Metro channels of Indian TV - the channel which is seen only. in the four major cities of Delhi, Calcutta, Bombay and Madras. Some big newspapers which already have TV or video experience are expected to be among the first group of people who will be allotted time and it would be interesting to watch how the competition provided by them lends keenness and fairness to the main Doordarshan channel which will still continue to be under the government.

The principle that the government cannot be identified with the ruling party nor with the individual ministers is difficult to implement although it is implicit in the democratic system. The party in power has to recognise the rights of the other parties and. has to realise that it can one day go out of power. The Congress party which has ruled India for most of the time since 'the nation acquired its freedom in 1947 has twice been defeated, in 1977 and again in 1989. So there is no irreplacability insofar as political parties are concerned.

The mediamen also have a major responsibility to present fair and objective news coverage in their bulletins and produce credible current affairs programmes. Admittedly, they function under a great deal of pressure and oral instructions are handed out to them for distorting the news. If they do not comply, they stand to suffer in their careers. They can be transferred to unpleasant assignments at short notice and since there are others ready to take their place they fall in the esteem of their peers. At least they think so and many of their colleagues think likewise. The search is always on for pliable chiefs who will not have many qualms of conscience.

The pliability must give way to a mixture of firm adherence to one's media responsibility and pragmatism. The latter will help them to make adjustments on comparatively less important matters while the former will ensure that their bulletins are fair and objective. The habit of playing up to the political masters to earn favours for the present and futures must change.

Not only the mediamen have to learn not to do things against their media conscience but the permanent bureaucrats who help the conscience but the permanent bureaucrats who help the ministers run the affairs of government also have to act as true civil servants. They must have the courage to tell their ministers that certain things just cannot be done. They have to protect the media people and act as cushions between the political masters who are demanding too much and the media people who may be trying to do their duty.

At present, the top civil servants act only as the mouthpieces of the ministers and make life miserable for the media people. Many of the latter also opt for the line of least resistance and the media, for all they care, can go to hell.

The media chiefs have to protect their editors and reporters and become the kind of cushion that the civil servants have to become between the media chiefs and the ministers, insofar as their relations with their performing subordinates are concerned. The latter have to be given a free hand to shape their coverage with some guidance in their work. They, in turn, have to be fully involved in the job and not act as mere implementers of orders or as official mediamen. The responsibility towards the listeners that we have spoken of again and again should be their major guide.

It would be easy to preach the doctrine of fearlessness and the media people would be justified in retorting "it is easier said than done." But a certain amount of fearlessness is essential along with the ability to take the rap when and if it comes, instead of passing the buck to one's subordinate, usually to the junior man who gets transferred to a remote "punishment" station. No wonder, some of the junior people are even more 'safety first' conscious than their bosses.

But that is hardly the kind of attitude they should show. It is they who have to uphold the credibility of their media. No doubt, the radio and TV editor is often the man in the middle and his head is the first to roll when the political bosses are angry. But the fear instinct should not become his mainspring for action and guide him in his daily work. There are many many intrepid men and women who have weathered storms time and again in the discharge of their duties and fulfilment of their media responsibility.

These people have to be protected and nurtured so that the media can play their role and serve the listeners truly and well.

The portrayal of the media situation in this chapter should not discourage the budding broadcast journalists seeking to enter the radio and TV and make a career with either of them. The problems of credibility have been dealt with a great measure of frankness so that they know what they would encounter in several of these countries and the kind of problems they would have to face.

The discussion that has preceded is not intended to dishearten them. A peep into the realities should actually equip them to meet the challenges and find some answers when they are face to face with the problems of media credibility.

The young broadcast journalists have to learn to adjust themselves to the situation and that does not mean they have to make compromises with the principles of broadcast journalism. All that we have elaborated in the pages of this book should actually stand them in good stead as they enter their chosen avocation. They would go into the business of newswriting secure in the knowledge that there are both challenges to be faced and thrills to be experienced in their job.

Make no mistake, the broadcast journalist's career is an exciting one. The journey becomes all the more interesting if the road is not entirely a smooth one and some difficulties could also arise.

Things in the media are bound to improve. They cannot but get better.

EXERCISES:

1. Write on the importance of media credibility and factuality.
2. Can the media discharge their duty to the listeners if they do not enjoy freedom to function?
3. What should the men in the media do to fulfil their responsibility to the audience in the situation that obtains in the radio and TV organisations of South and South East Asia?

Appendix A

BOOKS FOR FURTHER READING

1. *The Indian Reporter's Guide,* Richard Critchfield, Allied Publishing, Bombay.
2. *Editing: A Handbook for Journalists,* T.J.S. George, Indian Institute of Mass Communication (IIMC), New Delhi.
3. *Here's the News,* Compiled and Edited by Paul D. Maeseneer, Asian Books, New Delhi.
4. *Writing News for Broadcast,* Edward Bliss Jr. and John M. Patterson, Columbia University Press, New York.
5. *Deciding What's News,* Herbet J. Gans, Constable, London.
6. *Newsgathering,* Daniel R. Williamson, Hastings House, New York.
7. *News That Matters* Shanto Iyengar and Donald R. Kinder, University of Chicago Press, Chicago and London.
8. *Editing the Electronic Era,* Martin L. Gibson, Prentice Hall. New Delhi.
9. *Home Truths about Foreign News* Ed Harriman, Zee Books, London.
10. *Putting Reality Together: BBC News,* Philip Schlesinger, Methuen, London.
11. *News at Any Cost,* Tom Goldstein, Simon and Schuster, New York.
12. *Editing the News,* Roy H. Copperud and Ran Palnelson. WMC, Brown, Iowa.
13. *Broadcast / Cable Copyuiriting,* Peter B. Orlik, Allen and Bacon, London.
14. *Study of Punjabi News Bulletins.* lIMC, New Delhi.

15. *News Reporting and Writing,* Brian S. Brooks, St. Martin Press, New York.

16. *Professional Journalism,* Patanjali Sethi. Orient Longman, New Delhi.

17. *News Editing in the 80's,* William L. Rivers. Wadsworth Publishing, California.

18. *News Editing,* Bruce Westley, Oxford and IBH, New Delhi.

19. *IPI Manual on Techniques of News Editing, Sub-Editing Active Newsroom.* IPI (International Press Institute), Zurich.

20. *Politics of News: Third World Perspectives,* Jaswant S. Yadava, Concept Publishing, New Delhi.

21. *International Flow of News: An Annotated Bibliography,* edited by Hamid Mowlana. Nesco , Paris.

22. *Modern News Library,* Geoffrey Whatmore, Library Association, London.

23. *Television News: Interview,* Akiba R. Cohen, Sage, New Delhi.

24. *Poor Reception: Misunderstanding and Forgetting Broadcast News,* Barrie Gunter, Lawrence Erlbaum, London.

25. *International Handbook of Broadcasting Systems.* Philip T. Rosen, Irwin Illinois.

26. *Autonomy for the Electronic Media; A National Debate on the Prasar Bharato Bill,* T.K. Thomas, Konark Publishers, New Delhi.

27. *Themes in Indian Communication,* edited by M.R. Dua. Metropolitan Book company, Delhi.

28. *The Elements of Style,* William Strunk Jr. and E.B. White. The Macmillan Company, New York.

29. *Modern English Usage.* H.W. Fowler, Oxford University Press.

30. *The King's English* H.W. Fowler and F.G Fowler, Oxford University Press.

Appendix B

SELECTED PREPOSITIONS - MISTAKES TO BE AVOIDED

Abstain	*from*	-	not to participate, in a vote, for example. It does not mean being absent.
Admit	*to*	-	The accused admitted *to* the murder of his wife.
Agree	*to*	-	not *for.* "The two countries agreed *to* a non-agression pact".
Compare	*with*	-	not *to*. "This represents a four per cent increase in production as compared *with* the output last year."
Charged	*with*	-	not *for.* "The opposition charged the government *with* failure to maintain law and order." But accuded *of.* "The police have accused the suspect *of* robbery."
Congratulate	*on*	-	not *for.* "The captain congratulated the batsman *on* his century in the match."
Conform	*to*	-	but in conformity *with*.
Consist	*of*	-	but not comprise *of.* Avoid using "comprise" in the news. "The committee consists *of* four senior officers." If you have to use comprise, say, "the committee comprises four senior officers."

Cost. Discuss, Mention,		-	These verbs take no preposition. "This pair of shoes has cost me four hundred rupees." As a noun cost takes the preposition *of.* "He took three wickets at a cost *of* 15 runs each." *Discuss* must be followed by the object. "We discussed the weather, among other things." No preposition is required, but the object must be there. "The talks lasted two hours". Not lasted *for.* There are other verbs which take no preposition. Appointed, for example "He was appointed poet laureate" not appointed *as.*
Engaged in			to be engaged in some activity. "He was engaged in voluntary work for several years." But engaged *to,* to be married.
Flee	*from*	-	It is also used without a preposition. "The smuggler fled the country."
Emphasise, stress		-	No preposition when used as verbs. "The Finance Minister emphasised the need for fiscal discipline." When emphasis, or stress, is used as a noun the preposition *on* must be used. "The Finance Minister laid emphasis, or stress, on the need...
Inquire	*into*	-	also inquiry *into.* But *investigate,* generally used as a synonym, takes no preposition. "The police are investigating the murder of the actor."

Meet	-	needs no preposition. "The Prime Minister met today the visiting Malaysian Foreign Minister." But the American practice of saying "met *with* is being followed by many.
Laugh	*at, with* -	laugh at means ridicule, "The economist laughed at the suggestion for devaluation. "Laugh *with* means to join in the laughter. As the saying goes, "laugh and the world will laugh *with* you, cry and the world will laugh *at* you."
Pleased	*with*	
Rejoice	*at*	
Translate	*into* -	from another language. "The English text of the agreement was translated *into* Hindi."
Warn	*of* -	but the object must be placed next to the verb. "The Prime Minister warned the nation *of* the danger of complacency." You can also say "The Prime Minister warned the nation *against* the danger.." *Warn tell, inform assure,* must be followed by the person or group warned, assured, told, or informed.

Appendix C

LONG AND DIFFICULT WORDS TO BE AVOIDED

This is only an illustrative list

Avoid	**Use**
As regards In regard to Apropos of	About
Constituted	set up
Incarceration	jailed, put in prison
Implementation	carried out
Inauguration	opening
Insomnia	lack of sleep
Lackadaisical	indifferent
Lack-lustre	dull
Mediocre	ordinary, average
Melancholy	sad, gloomy
Melee	hand-to-hand fight
Negotiations	talks
Parsimonious	miserly
Procrastination	delay
Procreation	giving birth to
Necessitate	make necessary
Pusillanimity	timidity
Obdurate	obstinate
Prolix	lengthy

Reminiscences	memories
Remiss	careless
Renounce	give up
Repository	storehouse
Repugnance	aversion
Resurrection	raising a forgotton subject
Reverberate	echo
Seclusion	being alone
Stringent	strict
Utilise	use

Appendix D

AN HOURLY BULLETIN - A SAMPLE

All India Radio
News Services Division
English - 1200 HRS
KM.N. Mishra: Bhalla

5th December, 1992
This is all India Radio: The News Read by:

The Security arrangements in and around the disputed structure in Ayodhya have been beefed up, for the proposed "kar seva" to commence from tomorrow.

Thirteen more companies of the PAC have been deployed there and metal-detectors installed at different entry points in the complex.

The Centre has offered to place a squad each of bomb disposal and sniffer dogs for strengthening the arrangements.

According to the Home Ministry, the State government has accepted the offer.

Police and security agencies in Delhi also have been put on maximum alert to prevent any fallout of the kar seva in Ayodhya.

* * *

The News Services Division of All India Radio will broadcast a special programme on the Ayodhya issue today.

The half an hour programme will be available on Delhi "A" that is 366.3 metres from 9.30 tonight. It will also be available on .additional frequencies. Consequently, the National Programme of Music will Begin at 10.00 P.M.

The English News bulletin at 11.00 P.M. and the Hindi News

bulletin at 11.05 P.M. will be broadcast at 11.30 and 11.35 P.M.

* * *

In Haryana, the dreaded militant Hameet Singh Bahuwal alias Tochi was among the four killed in an encounter with the police in District Yamunanagar this morning.

According to an official spokesman, the police on a tip off, raided village Kunthala, in Radaur area this morning and in the ensuing encounter, Tochi, his wife and son and another accomplice were killed.

Tochi was responsible for over 150 killings in Punjab and Haryana including that of the Haryana Chief Ministers' OSD, Mr. M.L. Verma and his family.

He carried an award of ten lakh rupees on his head.

* * *

In Punjab, SIX militants including two hardcore were killed in separate encounters with security forces early this morning. According to an official spokesman, one hardcore Reshman Singh and two of his accomplices were killed in an encounter at a Village in MANSA district.

Some arms and other ammunition were recovered.

In another encounter one hardcore militant Tejinder Singh was killed in Hoshiarpur district.

In Amritsar district, two militants were killed.

* * *

The President has nominated SIX new members to the managing body of Indian Red Cross Society. They are Mother Teresa, Field Marshal S.H.F.J. Manekshaw, the former Chief Justice of India, Mr. Ranganath Mishra, Begum Bilkees Latif, Dr. B.V.K. Goel and the Union Health Secretary. The nominations have been made by Dr. Shankar Dayal Sharma in his capacity as the President of the Indian Red Cross Society. The Union Health Minister will be the Chairman of the Managing Committee of the Society.

* * *

The T'ripura Government has constituted a three-member high power Review Committee to look into complaints of unjustified dismissals of agitating policemen under Article 311. It will be headed by the State Chief Secretary, Mr. Damodaran. The Government decided to institute the Committee following large scale complaints from police personnel who were dismissed from service during the November agitation this year.

* * *

Mr Nitin Desai of India has been appointed as Under Secretary General for Policy Coordination and Sustainable Development, a newly created department of the United Nations.

This was announced the U.N. Secretary. General, Dr. Boutras Ghali.

Mr Desai has been the Chief Economic Adviser in Finance Ministry.

He was also actively associated with the Earth Summit held in Brazil this year.

* * *

Iraq says it is willing to restore relations with Arab countries who sided with the anti-Baghdad coalition during the Gulf War. In a statement in Baghdad the Iraqi' Vice President Mr. Taha Yassin Ramadan said that divisions between Arabs can not exist for an indefinite period and Iraq is ready to take a positive stand towards these countries.

Egypt, Saudi Arabia and Syria were the main Arab members who went against Iraq during the Gulf crisis.

Baghdad broke off its diplomatic relations with Cairo and Jeddah.

* * *

The Spanish Navy is battling to contain the massive oil slick spread· on the country's North-West coast. The slick which is nearly 30 kilometres long and more than a kilometre wide was caused when a Greek oil tanker ran aground in a storm on Thursday. The enormous oil fire generated by the accident has been put out.

But Spanish authorities say nearly thirty square kilometres area along Spain's coastline is faced with an ecological catastrophe.

* * *

That is the end of this news bulletin.

Appendix E

A REGIONAL NEWS BULLETIN - A SAMPLE

Morning Regional News Bulletin:

CRD:NR:JKES:

Date 11.12.92

This is All India Radio Shillong

The Regional News Read By -

Page: 1

Item No:1

Saikia

The Assam Chief Minister, Mr Hiteswar Saikia yesterday visited curfew-bound areas of Goalpara and directed the District Administration to immediately constitute a peace committee to maintain harmony. He also addressed leading citizens of Goalpara town and urged the people to maintain peace and harmony at all costs. Mr Saikia visited Harisabha, Sanibari, Mandir, Kamakhya Udyog and Thakurbari areas in Goalpara town which were attacked by miscreants. He also visited curfew-bound Lakhipur town and met a cross-section of the people and appealed to them to maintain peace and harmony.

(UNI/JK)

No.3

R.K.

The Manipur Chief Minister, Mr. R.K. Dorendra Singh has expressed solidarity and support to the Prime Minister Mr. P.V. Narasimha Rao. He has appealed to all secular and nationalist forces in the country to strengthen the hands of the Prime Minister in fighting challenges posed by communal and divisive forces. Mr Singh condemned the destruction of the mosque at Ayodhya. He appealed to the people to act with patience and help the Prime Minister in tiding over the crisis.

(UNI/CR)

No.6

NEHU-KSU

A Press Release issued by the North Eastern Rill University says that an understanding has been reached between NEHU officials and KSU leaders beginning a relationship of reconciliation and mutual co-operation. This follows the incident at Bijni Complex on the 28th of last month. The memorandum of understanding was signed by the General Secretary of the KSU and the Registrar of the NEHU in the presence of the Vice-Chancellor, NEHU and a modest gathering of KSU office-bearers. NEHU officials, members of NEHU faculty and office-bearers of Synjuk Ki Seng Samla Shnong, were the special invitees. The meeting was chaired by the Chief Proctor Prof. Milton S. Sangma. The gathering was addressed by Prof. M.S. Sangma, Prof. M. Lyngrah, Mr. Paul Lyngdoh and Prof M.K. Choudury. The ceremony ended with a brief speech and a vote of thanks by Prof. B. Pakem, the Vice Chancellor of NEHU.

(JK)

No.4

CONCERN

The Hill State People's Democratic Party and the Public Demands Implementation Convention have expressed grave concern over the prevailing law and order situation in some parts of the country following Sunday's incidents at Ayodhya. The HSPDP regretted the failure of the Central and the U.P. Governments to take timely steps to prevent the unfortunate incidents. The PDIC's Political Affairs Committee appealed to the Prime Minister to punish the guilty. Both parties have urged the people of the country to maintain peace and communal harmony.

(JK)

No.5

MUSLIM

A meeting of the elders of the Muslim community of Shillong was held yesterday to discuss the fall out of the demolition of the Babri Mosque. In a resolution adopted at the Meeting, the elders appealed to the Muslims to exercise utmost restraint and not to be provoked by provocative acts.

(JK)

No.7

NEHU

The Meghalaya Governor Mr Madhukar Dighe, visited the NEHU permanent Campus at Mawlai-Umshing on Wednesday. Mr Dighe inspected the facilities in the new building and the students hostels. He formally named the hostels. One of the hostels that he has named is Saramati after the highest mountain in Nagaland, another is Japfu after another high peak overlooking Kohima, the third one, Sohpetbneng after the high hill in the Khasi Hills where Khasis are said to have first settled and the fourth one as Chinlung after the original home of the Chin-Mizo people. He also visited the new Science Complex. On the occasion, Mr Madhukar Dighe assured the university of all possible help for its development. The Vice Chancellor expressed his gratitude to him for his concern for the development of the University.

(NR)

No.8

DIED

The retired Chief Engineer of Assam PWD, Mr Habibuddin Ahmed passed away at his Laban residence in Shillong on Wednesday following illness. He was 82. His burial will take place today in the Lumparing Muslim Grave Yard.

(NR)

No. 10

FUNCTION

The annual function of the Stephen Memorial School was held in Shillong yesterday. The Meghalaya Director of Sports, Mr. W.S.

Mawlong was the Chief Guest. He announced a grant of thirty thousand rupees for developing the school's basketball complex. Students also presented an entertainment programme on the occasion.

(JK)

No.9

WANGALA

The Wangala Dance and the Cultural Festival of the North Eastern Zone Cultural group will be held on Sunday and Wednesday at Tura. The venue will be the Chandmari playground. This has been stated in a Press Release issued in Shillong.

(JK)

No.2

ASSAM

Meanwhile the overall situation was reported to be tense but under control yesterday. The death toll rose to 76 with recovery of more dead bodies. Curfew, however, was still in force in some of the troubled areas as a precautionary measure. Army jawans were guarding sensitive places for the third day to prevent any untoward incident. The death toll following the Ayodhya development and Bharat bandh rose to 76 with the recovery of four bodies from a pond in Pathuri village in Nagaon district. The situation in Cachar, Karimganj and Hailakandi districts of Barak valley in South Assam is limping back to normal. The curfew, which was imposed only in Silchar town was relaxed for two hours from 11 A.M. There was no report of violence.

(PTI/CR)

That is the end of the News.

Note: The regional news bulletins from different AIR stations and in the Indian languages spoken in the states concerned. The morning regional news bulletin from AIR Shillong, reproduced above, is the only one in English.

INDEX